Victorian Cottage Rugs

How to Hook
16 Traditional Patterns

Pat Hornafius

with illustrations by Kay Carter Rader

STACKPOLE
BOOKS

Published by
STACKPOLE BOOKS
5067 Ritter Road
Mechanicsburg, PA 17055

Cover Design by Kay Carter Rader

IMPORTANT NOTICE TO READERS
This book is intended to be used by rug hookers for the creation of their own rugs and not by rug hookers or others for commercial exploitation.

Dyeing can be dangerous. Read and observe all warnings and usage precautions on dye packaging materials. Neither the publisher nor the author can accept any liability for any consequences arising from the use of dyes.

Lace patterns derived from European lace pieces in the Textile Collection of the Museum of Fine Arts, Boston. Adaptations by designer Ingrid K. Ziegler. Reproduced by permission of the Museum of Fine Arts, Boston.

Printed in the United States of America

First Edition
10 9 8 7 6 5 4 3 2 1

Library of Congress Cataloging-in-Publication Data
Hornafius, Pat.
    Victorian cottage rugs : how to hook 16 traditional patterns / Pat Hornafius. — 1st ed.
        p.   cm.
    Includes index.
    ISBN 0-8117-2593-6
    1. Rugs, Hooked—United States.   2. Rugs, Hooked—United States—Patterns.   3. Decorative arts, Victorian—United States. I. Title.
TT850.H674   1995
746.7'4—dc20   94-41929
                                                            CIP

Contents

Acknowledgments

To my colleagues in dyeing who helped me over the hurdle of switching from Cushing union dyes to acid dyes, I give bountiful thanks. Jane Olson and Elin Noble were graciously available for advice, instruction, and panic calls. To Maryanne Lincoln, I am profoundly indebted for the dye workshops and selfless sharing of her talent and expertise in formulating dye colors and dyeing with acid dyes. To my friends at PRO Chemical & Dye, Inc. who led me into WashFast acid dyes, thanks for all of the time and effort.

A special thanks to my students Mary Floyd and Barbara Pirtle, who submitted their beautiful work for photography, and to Greg Heisey of Foto Fast, Lancaster, Pennsylvania, for the fine photography.

Many thanks to Kay Carter Rader for her clear and concise illustrations.

To Sally Atwater, my editor, a patient source of help and encouragement, a sincere thank you. The Elizabethtown Public Library again was a source of Victorian research. To my husband, Jack, who photographed some of the rugs for this publication, and my daughter, Carrie Freeman, who worked typing and retyping the manuscript into her busy schedule, I extend my love and appreciation for the invaluable help.

Dear Reader,

For those of you who have enjoyed *Country Rugs,* read on! *Victorian Cottage Rugs* not only has sixteen new patterns, but also introduces the rug maker to new techniques, new dye discoveries, and new equipment.

Faithful fans—keep writing to me. From the artist who turned my designs into tiny dollhouse rugs (with French knots) to the purist who hooked her primitive rug with a bent nail, I love hearing from all of you.

Happy Hooking,
Pat

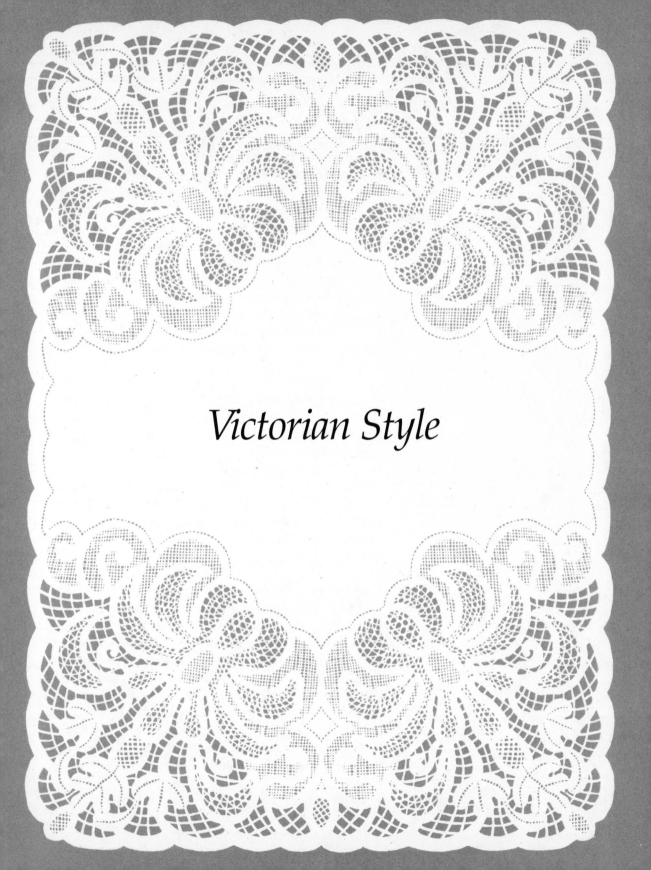

Victorian Style

Victorian revival! The lush exuberance of Victorian decor, coupled with twentieth century restraint, has made our homes cozy again. The appeal of a warm, inviting environment to come home to from the cold, sterile workplace has made the Victorian Cottage style popular today.

This is not the dark, plush, formal decor of your grandmother's day, but a light, cheerful, romantic, and informal style. Flowered chintz covers comfortable, soft-cushioned furniture, and the rooms are adorned with hand-crafted accessories.

The Victorian love of animals is echoed in paintings, needlepoint pillows, and hooked rugs. Faithful friend or endangered species—we create hearth rugs to commemorate them.

Love of home and friends is as important today as it was to the Victorians. These sentiments are echoed in "Welcome" rugs and the slogan that typifies the era, "Home Sweet Home." Embroidered on pictures and pillows, and hooked into rugs, this phrase is the summation of Victorian attitudes.

Nature is brought inside in the form of twig and wicker furniture, baskets, shells, wreaths, and plants. All these decorative motifs can be found on hooked rugs reflecting the Victorian Country style—romantic, comfortable, and cozy.

The Victorian Era

The first Victorian era covered a span of sixty-nine years, the reign of Queen Victoria (1832–1901). Though we tend to lump them all together, this period actually encompassed several styles in color and design, from the light, classic look of Regency with its graceful furniture and pastel colors to the heavy baroque embellishments and deep, rich colors of the late 1800s, brought on by the wealth and technology of the Industrial Revolution. The rug designs shown in *Victorian Cottage Rugs* fall in somewhere in the middle of this long period.

Victorian Cottage Architecture

While Queen Victoria engendered an age, Andrew Jackson Downing created in the mid-nineteenth century a style for America—Victorian Cottage—in his many books on house and garden design, which urged gentrification of the rising middle class.

Rebelling against the formality and symmetry of Federal architecture, with its Greek influences (Classic Revival), Downing designed houses that favored the individualism of Gothic architecture, translating its stylistic elements into wood. The invention of the power scroll saw enabled workmen to render the stone traceries of Gothic cathedrals in wood; this was known as "gingerbread" trim. Turned spindles and finials, fanciful cutouts, and ornamental swags graced houses both inside and out. Pointed windows, steeply pitched roofs, turrets, large windows, and verandas were typical elements of this movement. A combination of shingles, clapboard siding, stained glass, and scrolled wood ornamentation decorated these "cottages," which ranged from small suburban dwellings to palatial country mansions.

The flight to the suburbs from the crowded cities became possible at midcentury with the development of train service and streetcars with their more frequent stops. This enabled businessmen to live farther from town in gracious planned neighborhoods with people of similar incomes and similar tastes in houses.

Downing spearheaded the ideal of suburbia. His books promoted cottage residences, romantic designs inexpensively detailed in wood. His houses were sentimental, full of "feeling," sheltered from the storm of life. Snug and cozy, small and affordable, Victorian cottages sprang up all over the land, even being offered by mail-order companies to settlers in the West.

Victorian Gardens

The surrounding gardens reflected the colorful informality of cottage architecture. Carpenter Gothic paralleled the development of the informal "English" garden. A horticulturist as well as an architect, Downing urged that the romantic look extend from the house to the garden to create a "vista." The verandas surrounding the house (and the accompanying rocking chairs) provided a transition from the inside to the outdoors to better view the plantings (and the neighbors).

Flowers, because they are nonessential, were considered a luxury, so flower gardens became important as a sign of prosperity and a measure of the leisure time that was required to grow them, showing the world a home of beauty and gentility.

From Farm to Town

Rug making, basically a craft for the middle class, moved from farm to cottage with ease. Women in small towns retained their country skills. Given more leisure time, aniline dyes, and commercial patterns and materials, these women changed the primitive hand-drawn look of their predecessors' hooked rugs to a more sophisticated version, reflecting current styles rather than using motifs drawn from life on the farm. Home decorating was a favorite topic of ladies' magazines, and needlework was an outlet for women's creativity. Patterns for hooked rugs appeared in publications along with embroidery, needlepoint, and other textile crafts.

The History of Commercial Patterns

After the Civil War in 1865, Edward Sands Frost, an itinerant Maine peddler, fabricated a method of stenciling rug patterns onto new burlap, replacing the hand-drawn primitive versions marked on feedbag foundations. Printed in color and reflecting the new taste for fancy and floral designs, Frost patterns were an instant success. Frost opened a pattern shop, employing artists to translate the current fashionable motifs into hooked rug designs. His successor and many competitors poured out hundreds of patterns, but there was a market for all. Patterns were available through mail-order catalogs and at the general store. Floral designs with scrolls (translated from French Aubusson carpets), symbols of fraternal orders, and patriotic motifs appeared in rug patterns. Animals, always a favorite, remained popular, and adaptations of oriental patterns became the rage.

This is not to say that originality was dead. Women, who welcomed the time-saving innovations, often made their own versions of commercial patterns, choosing colors, rearranging motifs, and changing borders. Sharing and copying patterns were still common in sewing circles and church groups. The community of Victorian needlewomen gladly exchanged valued designs. Transmitted by pasteboard cutouts (I have some of these), tracings, and freehand adaptations, professionally drawn patterns were transposed into personal and individualized designs.

Victorian Design Preferences

The influence of English design and the preferences of Queen Victoria cannot be overstated. She not only ruled an empire, but set the standard for matters of home decor and demeanor. Her taste was middle-class, and the middle class on both sides of the Atlantic aped her preferences.

Although the process of rug hooking did not change from farm to town, colors, no longer limited to vegetable dyes, and designs, now commercially available, became more sophisticated. Leaving the simple farm motifs behind, Victorian women embellished their hooked rugs with fancy borders taken from other needlework sources, relinquishing the simple quilt designs and plain borders used in earlier rugs. Victorian scrolls and curlicues were found in all facets of design, from ironwork to typography, from house trim to hooked rugs.

The London Exhibition of 1851, held in the Crystal Palace, displayed fabulous products from all over the world and created a craze for anything exotic. These fanciful motifs were very soon adapted to home decor, and hooked rug patterns were not far behind.

Victorian Cottage Furniture

As early as 1830, catalogs advertised "cottage furniture," a scaled-down, simplified version of more expensive formal styles. Crafted in soft woods, cottage furniture was often painted in pastel shades or grained with sponged paint to imitate more costly woods. Bedroom suites had the additional embellishment of hand-painted or stenciled floral designs.

Hooked rugs were and are a perfect complement to Victorian cottage furniture. Small area rugs were used to warm the floor beside the bed and in front of the dressing table. Hooked runners for hallways and staircases and the rug under the dining room table could easily be lifted to clean and air or removed to clear the floor for children's games. This mobile informality was a necessity in an age before vacuum cleaners and moth proofing. Vermin were an ever-present scourge!

The Hearth Rug

Bare floors with small hooked area rugs in bedrooms and halls remained popular (and easy to clean) throughout the Victorian era. After the Civil War, wall-to-wall carpeting woven in strips became a basic necessity, laid over softwood subflooring to avoid the expense of finished hardwood floors. Wall-to-wall carpeting made hearth rugs essential to protect the large expanse from soil, sparks, and charring.

We cringe to think that handmade hearth rugs would serve such an ignoble purpose, but hooked rugs were not a sign of prosperity as was wall-to-wall Wilton. Some manufacturers provided matching hearth rugs to protect the parlor carpeting, but on the whole, hearth rugs gave vent to more handicraft on the part of the creative housewife and were a way to further embellish the center of family life. The hearth rug has a long history in decorating the "heart of the home," as the fireplace was a warm gathering place for family activities at the end of the day. Father read, Mother sewed, and the children played, in a perfect tableau of the "abode of love."

Material Sources

As earlier rug hookers used the ragbag and ragman for fabric sources, so did the ever-thrifty middle-class housewives of the Victorian era. Supplementing these traditional sources were the new bright wool and clothing remnants, which changed the color schemes of Victorian rugs.

The easy accessibility of wool remnants from New England textile mills made rug hooking an inexpensive craft. Mill ends were sold throughout the Northeast.

Victorian Colors

The discovery of aniline dyes in 1856 added new colors to the rug maker's palette. The brilliant magentas, reds, purples, and greens associated with Victorian decor were made possible by the new dye process, replacing the softer hues of natural dyes. Indigo blue, the last color to be replaced (1901) by synthetic dye, remained a natural color and was used for Union soldier uniforms. If you have ever wondered about the preponderance of blue in New England rugs, Yankee uniforms are the reason!

Commercial dyes sold in small packets in the general store allowed the rug maker to dye and overdye faded materials to be used in rugs, replacing the laborious natural dye process used in earlier times.

Vivid yarns from Germany used in Berlin work (embroidery on cards) also influenced the taste of color choices in home decor. Victorians enthusiastically embraced these rich colors available for the first time at affordable prices.

Today's Victorian cottage colors are soft and pleasing watered-down versions of the bright antique colors. Cabbage roses on ivory backgrounds or rich, handsome shades on black backgrounds now dominate the market in rugs and furnishings. Deep hues of burgundy and forest green have again become popular, replacing the earth tones of earlier primitive rugs. Cotton chintz, rather than formal damask or velvet, is the fabric of choice today, which perfectly complements the use of hooked rugs in cottage decor.

Dating Victorian Rugs

Hooked rugs made before the discovery of synthetic dyes (1856) can be dated by the use of natural dyes and salvage fabric. With an increase in prosperity, purchased mill ends and store-bought fabrics were employed to make the rugs. The economy of the ragbag was no longer essential. The brilliant hues of the new aniline colors were found in purchased fabric. Dyeing was rarely done at home, except for the overdyeing or tinting of faded materials. The use of these bright colors places a hooked rug in the second half of the nineteenth century.

The popularity of black, thought of as a fashionable color because of Queen Victoria's mourning wardrobe, replaced the "sad" colors of gray, brown, and tan used in earlier, naturally dyed backgrounds.

The introduction of Berlin needlework not only changed the color preferences of Victorian rug makers, but also introduced sentimental themes and ornate patterns crowded with details. These professionally drawn designs came to replace the hand-drawn motifs of earlier rugs.

Stag designs, reminiscent of the Scottish highlands, were a favorite Victorian motif. This Edward Sands Frost pattern is available from W. Cushing & Co.

The lion was a popular motif, symbolizing not only the Empire, but also, in this case, peace on earth.

Increased ornamentation also framed the rug design in later nineteenth-century rugs. Gone were the simple borders often drawn from quilt designs. Now, frames within frames surrounded the central motif, replete with scrolls, ribbons and bows, trellis work, or the ever-present roses. These motifs, incidentally, were also found in woodwork, ironwork, and etched glass.

Earlier rugs depicted objects from the rug maker's life. Victorian rug motifs included exotic animals, oriental designs, fashionable dogs, Thoroughbred horses, sporting themes (indicating leisure time), highland stags, and tartans (favored by Queen Victoria), replacing the down-home depictions of farm life. Perhaps the most popular rug subjects remained flowers, particularly roses, now rendered in more realistic detail and shading.

Not only were central motifs more refined, but they were placed in scenic backgrounds, creating a setting or picture. Lions in the jungle, stags in the forest, and horses pulling sleighs, sulkies, or carriages were common. Many of these designs were taken from Currier and Ives prints so popular in Victorian times. This was a vast change from the earlier rug-hooking style of primitive farm animals floating in space.

Slogans, mottoes, and homilies adapted from Berlin work or popular refrains and religious verses were also sources of Victorian rug designs. These sayings were meant to instill in the viewer's mind the sanctity of the home and the comfort found therein.

In today's Victorian-style hooked rugs, the overly embellished designs of the earlier age have been cleaned up and provide an elegant yet cozy approach to Victorian Revival, contributing to an interior in which you can curl up and enjoy all the comforts of home.

Getting Started

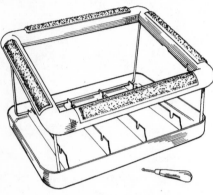

The Pittsburgh Crafting Frame is a lightweight lap frame that folds into its own case and is convenient for home use or travel.

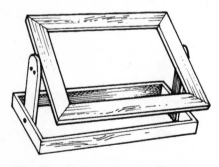

The Fraser Wooden Lap Frame is an inexpensive starter frame. The bars must be padded to accept T-pins to hold the pattern in place.

Equipment

To hook a rug, you will need the following equipment: a frame, a strip cutter, small to large hooks, and small, sharp scissors.

The Frame

There are many rug-hooking frames on the market. The newest and most convenient is the Pittsburgh Crafting Frame, an affordable, fully collapsible rug-hooking frame with permanently mounted gripper strips. The gripper strip construction keeps even the heaviest rug backing nice and tight. With a quick lift, the fabric pulls off immediately and is ready for repositioning by simply pulling it down over the frame again. Keeping your work tight makes it easier to locate holes and helps prevent crowded hooking and uneven loops. The Pittsburgh Crafting Frame sits squarely on your lap, is beautifully balanced, and allows both hands full access to your work area. It is completely rigid when locked into open position (16 by 13 inches, 7 inches high). It folds back into its own plastic case 2 inches deep and is lightweight, making it convenient for travel or storage. This is an extremely well-crafted frame with an ingenious collapsible all-in-one design. Used on a table top or placed on the lap, it does not need a stand.

The other lap frame I like is the Fraser Wooden Lap Frame. This is a comfortable, inexpensive, small (15 by 12 inches), and sturdy frame for tabletop or lap hooking. The wooden bars must be wrapped with toweling, or old blanket strips. This padding will accept angled T-pins to hold the rug foundation firmly in place. To move the work, remove the T-pins and reposition the pattern.

A more expensive lap frame that is best used with a stand is the Puritan Lap Frame. It has a 16-by-13-inch workspace. The gripper strips are mounted on bars that turn clockwise to tighten the work on the frame. To reposition the work, merely lift it from the frame, change the position of the rug, then tighten it again with the arms. Beware! Turning the arms counterclock-wise will break the spring and make the tightening mechanism ineffective. This is expensive to repair.

Quilt frames can be used as rug-hooking frames if they have an adjustable screw for enlarging the outer frame—hooked rugs are bulky. These quilt frames must have a stand. The Fraser Adjustable Frame is an easel-type frame that tilts to any angle and adjusts for height. The pattern is attached to the front and back bars, then tightened with ratchets positioned on each end. As the work is completed, it is rolled onto the bars.

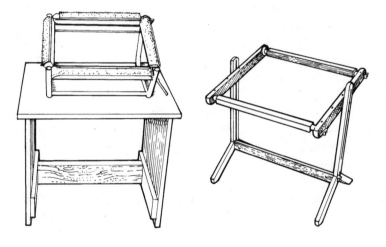

The Puritan Lap Frame (left) is best used on a sturdy stand. A simple low table can be inexpensively made at home to ensure the correct working height.

The Fraser Adjustable Frame can be tilted to any angle and adjusted for height. This is a frame and stand in one.

The Stand

A stand is optional. For those who do not have the space to have a hooked rug frame left out at all times and pre-fer tucking it away from family and friends, I would rec-ommend a tabletop lap frame. The Pittsburgh Crafting Frame mentioned earlier folds into its own carrying case and will fit into a closet. You must, of course, pro-vide a sturdy tabletop of the right type for a lap frame. The dining room table is too high; an old school desk is the perfect height and size. If you work in fits and starts (or in the car), no table or stand will be needed. Using such a frame on your lap works for a limited time, until the weight of it cuts off your circulation!

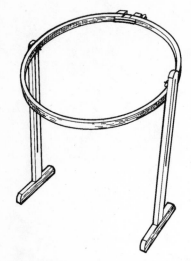

A quilt frame and stand can be used for rug hooking. Be sure to release the outer ring when not hooking to prevent creases in your work.

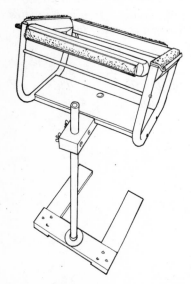

A homemade stand for a Puritan Lap Frame has footrests, and the frame can be turned to provide ease in hooking.

A sturdy stand will allow faster hooking and more even loops. Placing your feet in the footrests will keep the frame from bouncing around and make hooking fast, easy, and even. My first book, *Country Rugs,* gives a diagram of a Puritan Lap Frame stand that can be made by anyone who is handy.

The Strip Cutter

My designs in this book can be cut with a #6 cutting head if you must limit yourself to one blade. I prefer to use a #8 head for backgrounds (because hooking backgrounds bores me) and for all the dog designs in this book (because of the simplicity of their coats). Flowers are best hooked in small cuts (#4, #5, or #6) to allow more shading, as are leaves and small details. You can substitute #6 cut for the #8 cut described in my designs, but keep in mind that #6 cut requires three rows of hooking to occupy the same space as two rows of #8 cut. Many of my students prefer #6 cut for ease in hooking. Pulling up a 1/4-inch (#8 cut) strip, even on burlap, takes more tugging. The look using #6 cut will be a bit more refined and permits more detail.

The #6 cut will do everything I want it to do. It straddles the gap between wide cut primitive hooking and finer tapestry hooking. It is considered a wide cut but easily allows for four to six gradations of shading and does not put stress on tight foundations. Craftsman's Studio primitive linen is perfect for this cut, as is their primitive burlap with twelve holes to the square inch (see Sources). Harry M. Fraser Co. prints my patterns on monk's cloth or burlap, suitable for #6 and #8 cut strips.

The Victorian rugs in this book use strip widths from 1/4 inch (#8 cut) to 3/32 inch (#3 cut). Because of the variety of strip widths needed to get the Victorian look, a strip cutter is mandatory. It may be the best investment you ever make. Although hand cutting is fine for primitive rugs, it is almost impossible to keep on the grain of the fabric when cutting wool strips by hand,

and you will have fraying. Even though #6 and #8 cuts are considered primitive, the regularity of the machine cut strip outweighs the expense of the cutter.

I use the Bliss Strip Slitter Model A. This is a table model with suction cups to keep it from moving around when cutting the wool. The Fraser Model 500-1 is a clamp-on machine that will also take a cutting head for braided (or woven) rugs. Both use interchangeable cutting heads.

The cutting heads used in this book are #3 (cuts six strips $3/32$ inch wide), #4 (cuts four strips $1/8$ inch wide), #6 (cuts three strips $3/16$ inch wide), and #8 (cuts two strips $1/4$ inch wide).

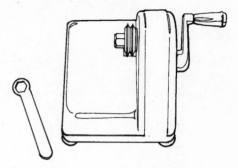

The Bliss Strip Slitter Model A sits on any surface to quickly cut your wool strips. Cutting heads are easily changed with an accompanying wrench.

The Hook

Hooks used in this book include a #2 primitive (used for hooking #8 cuts), a #3 hook (used for #6 cuts), and a #5 pencil-like hook for fine cuts. Use the handle shape that best suits your hand. My #2 ball-handled hook made my hand tired because I hook for hours at a time, so I had the sides flattened to fit my grip. I grasp a primitive hook like a baby clutches a spoon. When hooking with a pencil-like #5 hook for fine or medium strips, I hold the hook as I would a pencil. Different width strips require

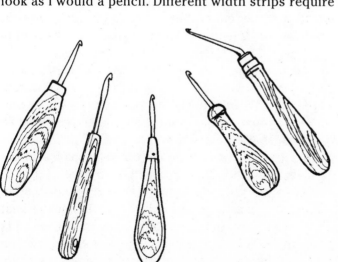

Hooks come in many sizes and shapes. Choose the handle best suited to your grip and the size of your strip.

different size hooks. It makes hooking that much easier. Not only will you hook faster and more evenly, but you will not put a strain on your hand and wrist.

Materials

The Foundation

The foundation material you use for your rug depends on the width or cut of the chosen wool strips and the desired fineness of the finished rug. The two go hand in hand. Wide strips ($^1/_4$ inch or #8 cut) limit the rug maker's shading capabilities, because wider cuts fill the space more quickly. I use four to six graduated shades of color in this book. Limiting shades to this number will achieve the Victorian look I strive for. This is not tapestry hooking, which can use up to twelve graduated shades, but a "primitive" approach to realistic shading. Finer cuts (#3 and #4) permit lifelike shading by the use of tiny widths and many graduated colors. I use these fine cuts for small details.

My approach is not that of a pencil drawing, but of a watercolor painting. Imagine that your hook is a brush, and use wider cuts where a wider brush would be employed, and finer cuts where a small brush would be appropriate. For those of you who paint, think of #3 cut as a striper brush for a very fine line or detail. The foundation is your canvas. If you plan to use very fine cuts, #3, #4, and #5 for the whole rug, choose a foundation with fewer holes to the square inch—linen or cotton.

Because #8 and #6 cuts ($^1/_4$- to $^3/_{16}$-inch-wide strips) are used throughout this book, as well as some #4 and #3, I recommend primitive linen, primitive burlap, or monk's cloth foundation material if you want to achieve the same look. I used primitive 10-ounce burlap for all of the pattern examples, skipping only one thread or mesh for #6 cut. The very fine cuts (#3, #4, and #5) used for details in some of the patterns will seem to float until loops around them pack them in. You may

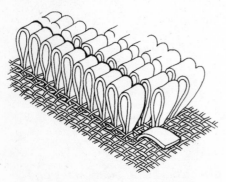

Wide strips of $^1/_4$ inch (#8 cut) require a more loosely woven foundation. Skip two threads between loops for even hooking.

even add some of these tiny details with #3, #4, or #5 cut strips when the area is completed.

The Wool

My favorite rug material is 100 percent wool flannel (12 ounces per yard). It has a close, even weave, suitable for all cuts, and dyes beautifully. Some wool flannel has a percentage of synthetic fiber woven in to give it more strength. This is acceptable if the synthetic is not more than 20 percent.

In general, the wider the cut, the thinner the wool can be. I use 12-ounce wool for #8 (1/4-inch) cuts because it slips through the mesh so easily. Pendleton wools are also this weight or even lighter.

Dorr and Woolrich wools are slightly heavier (13 to 14 ounces) and make a finer cut stronger. This is the standard wool used for tapestry hooking. Dorr and Woolrich wools also work well in #6 cut and even #8 (with a little more tugging and skipping two meshes).

Using Remnant Wools

There is nothing like finding plaid Pendleton trousers and slacks at the local thrift shop. I scout the January Goodwill sales for Christmas plaids donated from local men's shops. In the spring, thrift shops have wool specials. Be on the lookout for even-weave materials.

Tweeds, flannels, and plaids are wonderful additions to your fabric collection. Look for tightly woven materials—basket weaves fall apart. All my accents are overdyed tweeds and plaids, and although some color combinations are pretty awful, overdyeing them will solve the problem.

Plaids can be cut into their separate colors to be used as flower centers, leaf veins, and outlines as is or overdyed with the appropriate colors. Tweeds make great fur and feathers in hooked rugs but need to be shrunk to prevent falling apart. Avoid twills, gabardines, and other diagonally woven fabrics, as well as worsted wools used in men's suits; these all will fray.

I have never had luck with polyester blends. They

Measuring Your Wool

I often use ounces in this book to describe amounts of wool. You may be using ripped clothing (and I hope you are) or small remnants that cannot be measured in yardage. Weights of wool range from 14 ounces to 10 ounces, and dye amounts are consistent with wool weight, not yardage.

If you are purchasing 12-ounce white wool, the yardage requirements are as follows:
36 inches, or 1 yard = 12 ounces
27 inches, or 3/4 yard = 9 ounces
18 inches, or 1/2 yard = 6 ounces
9 inches, or 1/4 yard = 3 ounces
6 inches, or 1/6 yard = 2 ounces
3 inches, or 1/12 yard = 1 ounce

As most of my requirements fall within these measurements, you can readily make the conversion from ounces to yardage.

Use a small food or postage scale for weighing your wool. My scale has 1/2-ounce demarcations and weighs up to 5 pounds.

turn stiff when dyed at home and crumble when hooked. You may be tempted by the wonderful plaids, but pass them by. They are a disaster.

Woolrich plaids, 80 percent wool and 20 percent nylon, are a wonderful fabric to dye and to hook. Although it is wearing on your cutter blade, it makes a strong background.

Washing the Wool

Wool cloth, like a fine sweater, needs gentle care. Wash remnant wool from used clothing before cutting to rid the garment of cleaning fluids and soil. This will also plump up the fibers and make your loops more bouncy. I also rinse new yard goods (gently) in a warm soak, spinning out the fabric and fluffing it in the dryer, but not completely drying it. To complete the drying of your wool, hang it on a rack, shower curtain rod, or draped over the ironing board to avoid serious shrinkage or wrinkling.

Rapid changes of temperature and agitation will shrink and mat the wool. This is a good thing to remember when you need to tighten loose weaves (plaids and tweeds) that are too flimsy to cut into strips.

Do not iron your fabric before cutting it. This would press down the fibers you washed to create fluffiness.

When washing your wool, do not use strong detergents with added bleaching agents. Today, finding a detergent without bleaching agents is difficult. Hand soap or gentle dishwashing detergent will be the answer. Avoid at all costs a product that was formulated for hosiery, sweaters, and woolen garments. It contains bleaching agents that remove color. Also avoid fabric softener sheets and excessive water softeners; these form a film on the fabric that sticks to the cutter blade and makes cutting difficult.

Wool Requirements

When using a primitive cut (1/4 inch or #8 cut), four times the finished area will give you the required amount of wool. If using #6 or a finer cut, plan on five times the area. This additional yardage will take care of the wasted edge that should not be used when ripping the wool into strips. For ease in cutting, I try to tear my wool into 3- or 4-inch-wide strips, even wider for backgrounds that require a lot of material. This greater width (no wider than you can handle nicely on your strip cutter) saves yardage by eliminating extra torn edges that are weakened by ripping and should not be used. Save the first torn edge you cut in case of an emergency. The more strips that are torn, the more edges that are unusable.

No matter how carefully you plan, sometimes you will run short of a color. Redyeing a color, even when using the same dye formula, is not guaranteed to match the original shade. If you must add more wool to a hooked design, rip out several hooked strands here and there and replace these spots with the new dye lot. By mixing in the torn-out wool strips with the newly dyed batch, you can spread the color evenly throughout the area.

Tearing the Wool

Primitive rugs (#8 cut) can be torn with the selvage or from selvage to selvage across the weft of the material. The selvage is the finely woven edge running the length of the material along the two warp edges. Finer cuts (#6 on down), however, must be torn *with* the selvage in order to gain the strength of the warp threads (the threads running the length of the fabric). Measuring amounts of wool needed will become more difficult when tearing with the selvage to determine the length of each piece or color when dyeing. For each pattern, I indicate how to tear the wool to obtain the necessary strength for the cut of strips required.

Custom-dyed swatches from the hooked rug suppliers listed under Sources are generally 3 by 12 inches. For some colors, you will need lengths up to 27 inches. I list the lengths of the swatches needed in each pattern. If your purchased colors come in shorter lengths, buy a few more swatches to make up the ounce requirement.

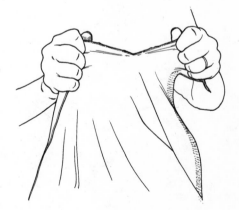

Tear the wool into strips with the selvage for #6 or finer cuts to gain the strength of the warp threads.

A 3-inch width of wool 57 inches wide is equal to 1 ounce of 12-ounce-weight wool. Using this standard, a 3-by-19-inch swatch is approximately 1/3 ounce of wool. Wool shrinks when being dyed. If you plan to dye your own wool and need many shades, add up your wool requirements in ounces. Figure out how many yards you need (12 ounces per yard for skirt weight, 13 to 14 ounces per yard for the slightly heavier Woolrich and Dorr wool); then make a paper chart of how you plan to tear your wool with the selvage, much like a cutting chart for laying out dress material on yardage needed to sew a garment.

This may sound complicated—and, frankly, it is—but colors can rarely be duplicated with today's acid dyes, so it is dangerous to run short while hooking. With a layout, when tearing with the selvage, you can determine the correct amount before ripping. Never use a piece shorter than 12 inches, unless you know that eyes, whiskers, or similar tiny areas will take up such small strips. Dorr Mill Store sells Quarter Yarders, 18-by-28 1/2-inch pieces that equal 3 ounces. This is a wonderful way to buy small pieces yet gain the needed length for strips.

In most cases, if you quadruple the area in wool that appears on the pattern, and add a little more for finer cuts, you will not run short.

Backgrounds are easy, as they use a yard or so of fabric and can be dyed in one large piece.

Cutting the Wool

If you purchase commercially dyed wool, determine if the fabric needs rinsing to be soft and bouncy for cutting. Hard-pressed dress goods will definitely need to be softened by rinsing. Hand-dyed swatches will be ready to cut.

You are now ready to cut the wool. I like to use the longest length possible (57 inches) for background hooking with #8 cut, torn from selvage to selvage. This may be awkward for novice rug makers. If you prefer to work with shorter strands, cut them in half (28 1/2 inches) or thirds (19 inches). Avoid as many cut ends (visible on

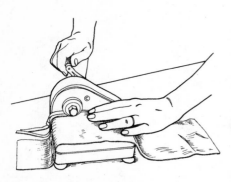

To cut the wool, guide it against the side and turn the handle. Different cutting blades will cut strips of varying widths.

the face of the rug) as possible; train yourself to use the longest strip that you can work with comfortably. Other lengths have been predetermined in the individual pattern instructions when torn for dyeing purposes *with the selvage* for #6 and finer cuts.

When cutting the wool for backgrounds, I like to use strips up to 4 inches wide to avoid waste. Always tear the wool to obtain the straight of the fabric. Unless you can follow the stripe of a plaid, do not cut the wool into strips for the strip cutter. Some plaids are sewn on the diagonal for flared skirts. If you are using dress remnants, be sure to tear these pieces to determine the straight grain.

Do not cut all the wool for a portion until you need it. If matching is necessary, a small uncut piece is easier to match than a little strip.

Bagging the Strips

After cutting half the required amount, place the strips in a sealable clear plastic bag, and use a permanent marker to label each with a number to correspond with your rug chart and cite the area to be hooked. Plastic grocery bags hold large amounts for the background and the various shades of color for different flowers, leaves, and borders.

Without organization, hooking with many colors, shades, and small strips is a nightmare. A curious pet, playful child, or stiff wind can make a maelstrom of hooking strips. I have dealt with all three. Plastic bags laid out on a side table can make finding the correct color very easy and controllable. Some rug hookers make muslin rolls to hold cut strips in graduated color sequence such as needlepoint or crewel embroiderers use. Others hang the strips on wooden racks or merely lay them out in order on a workspace.

For fine cuts, cardboard holders with serrated edges can display many shades of one color from light to dark. This is handy when using graduated strips of color. It is very difficult to determine small shifts in shades when they are all jumbled together. One to four shades or

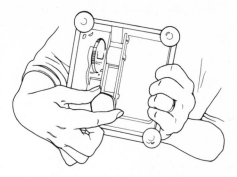

Tighten the pressure screw to adjust the tension of the cutting blade. Be sure to release the tension when the cutter is not in use.

even one to twelve shades are distinguishable at a glance when organized in cardboard keepers.

Use whatever system you have room for or find easiest, but definitely plan the quickest and most controlled way to handle your strips. It's important to be able to stop, store, and start again with as little time wasted as possible. Plastic bags do the job for me.

Making a Color Chart

This is important! Students always want to skip this simple step. To make a color chart, snip off a small piece of dyed wool (selvages are nice) for each color used in your rug, and glue it to a piece of paper or a page in a notebook. Then record the amount of wool required, the dye formula used, and where its placement is on the rug. This will avoid total confusion when hooking areas of many colors. The color chart should contain the formula used to obtain these shades or the purchased source, in case you need more of a color later.

Saving Your Scraps

I save all my scraps longer than 4 inches in a small box. My heritage is Pennsylvania German, and we are a thrifty people. But more important, these tiny pieces come in mighty handy when a flower center, small vein, or touch of color is needed. It eliminates having to dye a little strip. You will need this bit of color sometime. Waste not, want not!

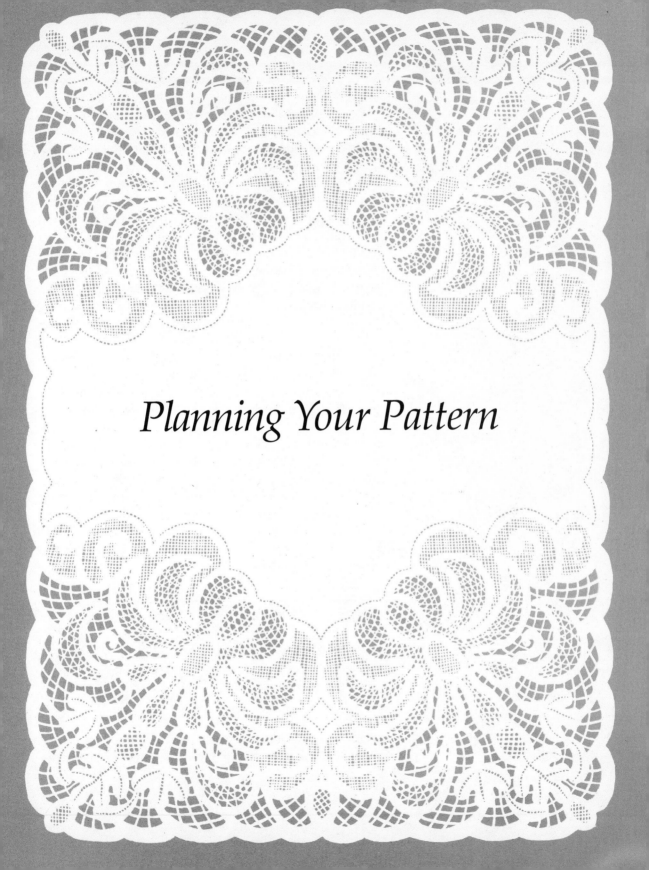

Planning Your Pattern

The intricacy of the pattern will be based on the number of holes in the foundation, the amount or degree of shading, and the complexity of the design.

Simple designs of animals and primitive flowers can be easily hooked on primitive burlap, primitive linen, or monk's cloth using #8 (1/4-inch) cut. More complex designs, however, with finer detail and graduated shading, can use a finer foundation. Primitive burlap, primitive linen, and monk's cloth will very easily accommodate #6 strips, hooked in every hole, or #8 strips, skipping two holes. Very finely cut details are difficult to hook directly on primitive burlap. When using burlap foundation, I hook cuts finer than #6 in their allotted spaces, then fill in around them at once. This will hold them in place. You can also add these tiny highlights after completing the whole area.

The patterns in this book range from simple to complex. There is something here for every range of hooking ability. Please feel free to interchange centers and borders—Edward Sands Frost did! Most patterns are based on a 2-by-3-foot format, which makes exchanging borders or creating your own center designs an easy matter. Harry M. Fraser Co. (see Sources), which now prints all my patterns, can print my designs on your choice of foundation material. If you choose to hook finer than I have indicated for each pattern, feel free to do so on the appropriate foundation.

Art Elements Applied to Rug Designs

Hooked rugs are works of art, and the basic elements of art—color, line, shape (space), and texture (patterns)—apply to rug design as well.

Color

Of all the art elements, color is the most important. When designing a hooked rug, you must determine where it will be used. Matching the decor is simple if you coordinate the rug with a printed fabric in the room. All printed fabrics have a color registration that appears on the selvage. These are the colors used in the printing and overprinting of the fabric, creating the pattern. Using wools dyed to match these basic colors (and shades thereof) ensures a pleasant color scheme that is guaranteed to match the decor.

Choosing the background color is the first consideration when designing your rug. Very light or very dark backgrounds work best. They contrast well with the middle tones used for the center of interest. On a dark background, keep the outer edges of the motifs light. On a light background, center the motifs with the lightest shades and move out to darker shades on the motifs' edges. This will keep the centers of interest sharp, preventing them from disappearing into the background.

Middle values are the most difficult choices for backgrounds. Unless you wish your rug to have an overall tone of even colors—and I have seen some lovely subtle designs that do this successfully—middle shades make the motifs disappear in the design. They make for unobtrusive rugs that can work well in the proper locations.

If the background is a medium value, be sure to outline the motifs touching the background in lighter or darker colors. *Never outline the objects in black or very dark colors.* This is harsh and jarring, even in the most primitive of rugs. A slightly darker or lighter shade will do the outlining job, blending in with the tones of the rest of the rug. Remember, a light or dark color for the background is a simpler choice as motif colors can be more easily discerned.

Planning the Color Scheme

I ask my students to make up a color chart before hooking a single loop. I also require that they start with the background color from which all other colors resonate. Knowing what you are doing before you begin will eliminate ripping out later. Lay the center-of-interest shades on the background wool. Then pile up pieces of your other colors surrounding the center in proportional amounts. How does it look? Too bright? Too dull? Do your colors fade away against each other or the background, or leap out too vigorously? Remember that every rug needs a bit of vivid contrast in the very smallest areas—eyes, leaf veins, flower centers—in order to bring them to life in the large expanse of your rug. Account for this tiny amount when laying your wools on the background color. Judge your colors on the floor for the long view. Up close, anything looks good. Do all the colors blend harmoniously? If not, *now* is the time to change things, not after you have hooked it in.

Are the colors properly spaced around the rug? I like to position the same hue in a triangular relationship throughout the rug to balance the color placement.

Trust your eye and make dyeing or color replacement choices before beginning to cut the wool for your rug. You will be glad you did.

In planning the rug, you must realize that colors have weight. Dark colors have more weight than light colors. This is a simple concept, but it is extremely important to the design of the rug.

Not only do dark colors have weight, but they also recede, creating visual "holes" in the rug. Be sure in planning your rug that these dark spots do not create eye-grabbing distractions. Every rug needs light, medium, and dark colors in unequal proportions. Light colors advance and pop out of a rug design, becoming visually larger than the surrounding areas. Colors that appear in the foreground of the others should be brighter; those behind should be duller to recede in space.

Line

Line in hooked rugs is created not only by the design, but also by the hooking direction. Wavy lines, Cs and Ss, and straight back-and-forth directional hooking all create patterns of their own. My rule of thumb is that the background hooking direction must enhance the center of interest. Sea or water motifs benefit by wavy hooking, as do most backgrounds. Simple centers of interest can take more intricate background directional hooking.

My favorite method of completing the background is to follow the outline of the central object, growing larger and larger until the curving directional hooking begins to flatten out at the border edges. This will allow for shadowing—using a slightly darker color around the central motif—or alternating subtle shades of the background color when filling in the field.

In primitive rug making, the hit-and-miss technique is often used to complete backgrounds. Various colors are chosen at random and are hooked in straight lines.

Shape

Shape, the central motif, and space, the resulting field, determine the design quality of your rug. Shapes that are too small for the size of the rug result in a weak design, whereas a large central motif creates a strong design. It is better to crowd the space, filling it with the central motif, than to have a small motif floating in space. Beginning designers often make this mistake.

Pattern or Texture

Tweeds, plaids, and checks all create textures of their own. They are wonderful when used with various shades of the same color. Primitive rugs, with their simpler motifs, benefit greatly from a variety of materials. Victorian rugs depend more on graduated values, using patterned fabrics for flower centers, leaves, borders, small areas, and defining lines.

Plaids and checks that are overdyed so that just a glimmer of the original pattern shows through create a marvelous background for animal motifs. Plaid fabrics can be cut into their various stripes of color, overdyeing light areas and using the dark areas separately, or overdyeing all for an interesting background.

In order to ensure a perfect design—and we all hate to rip out a rug—completely plan the color, line, shape, and texture of your rug pattern *before* you begin.

Designing Your Own Rug

It is fun and exciting to design your own rug. You may choose to hook your house surrounded by a border of flowers from your garden, duplicate a child's drawing, depict your children's favorite toys surrounded by a border of alphabet blocks, or use any other motif descriptive of your interests and your life. I recently designed a hooked rug of a school bus yellow Volkswagen Beetle that commemorates a client's first car. Your own hooked rug design can recall fond memories or depict cherished pets or objects.

Planning Your Design

I always make a thumbnail sketch of my rug idea. Use a 4-by-6-inch scrap of paper for your original design, then enlarge it proportionally as more ideas come to you. Having previously decided what size the finished rug will be, cut the paper pattern to the same proportion. For example, a 4-by-6-inch sketch can be perfectly enlarged to a 2-by-3-foot rug by increasing the finished paper design six times to 24 by 36 inches. The proportions of both measurements work out perfectly. Choose your rug's proportions and stick to them. Photographic enlargements are increased or decreased by percentages, so any proportional size is possible.

Plan your rug size first. Then determine the width of the border, if it will be an important element in the design of your rug. You will then know what space remains and how big the center motif will need to be. Working from the outside in may take some getting used to, but this "backward" method eliminates the need to juggle the border pattern later to fit the space. Help yourself to my border designs from any rug pattern in this book. I have designed most of the rugs in a 2-by-3-foot format for this reason.

Now place your motif in the center of the rug. You can borrow from my designs, change a dog or cat design to match your pet, or center your hobby in any appropriate border. Fill the space. Do not make the center motif too small, leaving too much space in the background. Filling the space will avoid an amateur look to your finished rug design.

Judging the Design

After making your basic sketch, before or after enlarging the whole, check your design for balance. Turn the design upside down and any odd spaces will immediately become apparent. The background, which will be filled with directional hooking, is considered a negative space; the center design is a positive space. These two must be in harmony, or your finished rug will be disappointing.

Enlarging a Design

You may need to enlarge or draw your central motif to fill the space pleasingly. A graphic arts shop can enlarge a drawing, photograph, or borrowed design to the exact size you request. Remember that the enlarging process is one of proportion. The picture is increased by percentage either photographically (expensive) or with a copier (inexpensive). Both processes of enlargement have size limitations. Find out beforehand what they are. I sometimes cut a design in sections and enlarge individual parts if the copier cannot handle my enlargement needs. Separate motifs can also be reduced using a copier. In this way, different motif sizes can be corrected to create a pleasing design. Cut out the motifs before transferring the design to the pattern paper. This will enable you to overlap forms.

If you are taking a photo of your house to be enlarged into a rug design, make things easier on yourself and take a straight-on shot. This will eliminate angled side walls, with their required shading. A dead-on photograph, or even better, an architect's front elevation, is easier to reproduce with strips of wool. Be sure your shot is a good one, as photographic enlargement cannot magically transform a bad photograph. Small details will be lost, but this makes hooking the house simpler.

Transferring the Design to the Pattern Paper

Now you are ready to draw a final copy of your intended design to the finished size. Use an inexpensive piece of paper, such as white butcher paper. This is the time to fiddle around with center motifs and border widths. Keep in mind that the more involved and detailed the border, the plainer the central motif should be, and vice versa. The eye needs some relief. Also keep in mind that the width of your hooking strips, #8 cut (¼-inch strips), cannot produce the detail that #6 cut or smaller width makes possible. More shading is possible with the finer strips, if that is your intent.

Next, assemble the entire rug design (center motif section and border sections, completed and corrected) under the material chosen for transfer.

Many of my students use a sheer pressed fabric interfacing called Pellon with a grid pattern, or Red Dot Tracer with a red dot grid. These semitransparent materials are strong, do not tear with the pressure of a pen, and can be traced through with a fine permanent marker.

Because of the large number of rug designs I make and transfer, I use a very inexpensive plastic film sold by farm suppliers and hardware stores. This 3-mil natural flat sheet polyethylene is soft, pliable, strong, and almost transparent, but it comes in large rolls (36 inches by 100 feet). It is so inexpensive that you will not regret buying a whole roll. I also use it to protect surfaces from moisture or paint and, yes, in the garden!

Another semitransparent material I have used for pattern paper is draftsman's parchment sold in rolls of different sizes in art shops. Strong and crisp, this paper does not slide around like plastic or fabric and can be easily taped to the foundation.

Fiberglass screen is a new addition to tracing materials. Flexible and strong screening in its various widths can be laid on top of a finished design and traced with a fine permanent marker to create an easily readable pattern.

All of the above pattern materials are semitransparent and strong. Tissue paper shreds when drawn on, so
don't use it. I position my different designs, center and
border, under the pattern paper and arrange them by
sliding them around until the space is filled to my lik-
ing. The pattern paper creates a "veil" that blends the
disparate sections into a unified whole, so that design
qualities are more readily apparent. When you have
adjusted the design elements under the transfer material, copy the perfected design onto it with a permanent
marking pen.

Tracing the Pattern

Enlarging the Pattern

If you are enlarging one of the patterns in this book, you will need to duplicate the grid on a piece of paper the chosen size. Transfer the lines as they are drawn in each of the squares onto your paper pattern. When you have arrived at the finished image, you will need to trace it onto the chosen foundation.

Enlarging a grid is not everybody's cup of tea. I prefer to go to a graphic arts shop that can photographically enlarge any size image to any percent. If you are designing your own rug, this method will enable you to enlarge or reduce any number of motifs to the correct size. A copy machine will do the same type of enlargement, but you are limited to the size of the paper the copier will hold. By cutting your design in pieces and enlarging them individually, you can then assemble the puzzle and tape your pattern together. Mechanical enlargements will be photographically crisp and clear; copier enlargements tend to get fuzzy as they are enlarged.

As an ex-schoolteacher, I have often used an opaque projector to enlarge a design. Pin up the paper you will use to trace on a wall, adjust the projector to the correct size (I always outline the perimeters of the finished rug size before projecting), then merely copy the exact image onto the pattern paper. A slide projector will do the same job, if you are fortunate enough to have a slide of your chosen design. Overhead projectors used in classrooms are another method of mechanically transferring your design to the pattern paper. They require a design drawn on clear acetate.

In all cases, prepare the size of the paper to your chosen dimensions, leave room for a border design, and trace these lines on the pattern before projecting your image.

Preparing the Foundation

When planning the amount of foundation fabric needed for your rug, always include a margin of at least 6 inches around the outside edges. This additional yardage will give you plenty of material to hem or zigzag to prevent fraying while working. It allows enough space around the perimeter of the rug to fit into your chosen frame and leaves a little extra for additional rows around the outside edge if you decide to add more border when the rug is finished. Additional rows sometimes enhance the completed rug design, and two outside rows are mandatory in case the edge becomes torn or ripped.

To prevent fraying of foundation fabrics, hem, overcast, or zigzag your edges before beginning to hook. On a cotton rug base, you may seal the edges with a coat of diluted white glue to prevent fraying while work is in progress. Be sure to brush on the thinned-out glue on a waxed paper underlay, or your pattern may become part of the counter!

Transferring the Design

After determining the size of the foundation, center the paper pattern on top of this material, allowing an outside margin of 6 inches. Measure in from the outside edges to be sure the pattern will be centered. The selvage is always a straight edge; cut edges must be on grain as well. Blue lines woven into monk's cloth will assist you in finding the straight of the fabric. On burlap, pull a thread on an outside edge to determine the grain if you are in doubt. It is very important when hooking to be sure that the pattern is traced on the straight of the material. It is worth all this extra work so that hooking straight lines will be very easy and automatic. Juggling around from one mesh to another when hooking a line is possible but very time-consuming.

To double-check for a perfect rectangle, use a carpenter's trick: Measure diagonally from one corner to another. Match this diagonal measurement in the other direction. If both measurements are the same, your rug perimeter will be perfect.

Transferring with Carbon Paper

Fasten the foundation to the tracing surface with masking tape, and draw the perimeters with permanent marker. Within the perimeters, lay down sheets of black carbon paper on the foundation material. Then lay the paper pattern on top. Fasten the pattern to the tracing surface with masking tape so that it will not move.

Use a hard surface for transferring the pattern. I use a laminated plastic table or, for large rugs, my dining room table covered with table pads. If you treasure your furniture, be sure to pad the surface well. Layers of newspaper will do. Whatever you plan to trace on, be sure it is large enough that you can completely lay out the entire design. Tracing piecemeal will dislodge your pattern.

Using a ballpoint pen, trace the pattern through the carbon onto the foundation. Press hard for a dark outline. Start in the center and work toward the outside edges. Before removing the pattern and tape, sneak a peek in one corner to determine the darkness of the line transfer. If it is not dark enough, without dislodging the pattern, retrace it. Remove the paper and carbon. At this point, I like to go over the lines with a fine permanent black marker. This permits any correction of the design and will prevent the lines from rubbing off with repeated handling of the work. Be sure to use permanent markers, because they are waterproof.

Transferring with Iron-On Pencil

If you prefer a transfer pencil that irons the lines onto the foundation, bear in mind that this method of transfer will reverse the design if drawn on top. If your pattern paper is transparent, you can draw with this pencil on the back of the design. Of course, if the design can be reversed without loss of clarity, draw on the front and turn over to press the pattern design onto the foundation material. I have never had success with iron-on transfer pencil on burlap, but try it on cotton or linen foundations.

Transferring with Tracer Material

Tracer material used for the final design makes tracing a simple task. My students who use interfacing pattern material for the final drawing trace over the lines with a fine permanent marking pen that bleeds through the mesh and eliminates the need for carbon paper.

Fiberglass window screening can do the same job. Trace the completed and corrected pattern onto the screening material, then retrace with a fine permanent marking pen to transfer the design onto the foundation fabric.

How to Hook

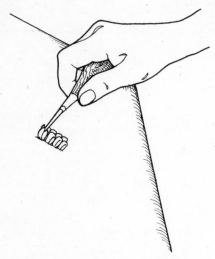

Grasp a primitive (#2) hook like a baby holds a spoon. This will make hooking with a ¼-inch strip less tiring to your hand and wrist.

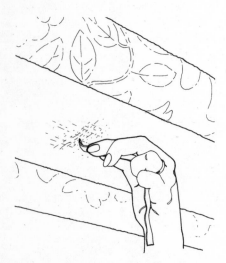

The left hand under the frame controls the strips and adjusts the height of the loops. To rip out a section, pull the strip down on the underside.

Pattern in hand and fabric prepared, you are now ready to hook. Place the foundation on the frame. With gripper strip type frames that make it possible to easily remove and readjust the pattern, merely tighten the foundation by pulling firmly against the carding strips. With quilt or easel type frames, tighten the pattern like a drum. The tension will increase as you fill in the holes, so allow a little play to begin with. A tight tension is essential, as it is difficult to hook evenly on a floppy surface.

Rug hooking is a very simple craft. For #6 and #8 cuts, the right hand clutches a primitive #2 hook like a baby holds a spoon. For narrower cuts, use smaller hooks and hold them like a pencil. These different grips will become comfortable with use and save your arm and hand from strain.

Begin hooking your design in the middle of the rug. Your aim is nice, fat loops, not squeezed together, about ¼ inch high. Using the right hand, thrust the hook through a hole in the mesh. The left hand, placed directly under the hook beneath the frame, holds the strip of wool and assists the strip onto the hook. Hold the strip with the left thumb and forefinger against the foundation material. The loop will be drawn up through the foundation about ¼ inch high, creating a pile. This is a consecutive motion. The upper hand controls the action of the hook and the height of the loop. The lower hand controls the strip. To rip out a loop or lower its height, merely pull down with the lower hand.

Using wide cuts (#8 or ¼ inch), I skip two threads of the weave between loops. This space prevents bunching and crowding, which would make the work lumpy and unable to lie flat on the floor. I also skip two rows of threads beside each #8 cut row. Insert your hook where it feels comfortable. It is not necessary to alternate mesh holes from one row to the next with a ¼-inch-wide strip. There will be some foundation showing behind the rug.

Working with #6 cut (³/₃₂ inch), skip only one thread of the mesh when using a 10-ounce burlap foundation. Tighter weaves may necessitate skipping two threads.

Use your judgment. Rug loops are held in place with judicious packing. If the work is not hooked closely enough, catching an end can pull out an entire row. Don't fret. You will soon get a gauge that lies flat, but does not pull out.

The evenness of the height of the loops will come with practice. I make all rugs with 1/4-inch-high loops regardless of the size of the cut. Since I do not do tapestry hooking with very fine cuts, I find that 1/4-inch-high loops provide a very nice pile and good wearing qualities.

When you complete a color or strip, clip the end 1/4 inch high as you go. This prevents having an unsightly bunch of straggly ends sticking up from the pile as you work. When clipping, to avoid missing the vagrant thread, I pull the last loop a bit higher and clip off the top of the entire loop, giving a completely clean cut to the wool. Some prefer to slip the small, sharp scissor points into the last loop to cut off the remaining strand. If this strip is not cut cleanly, however, it will tear out when the unused portion is pulled away.

Begin the next strand in the same hole. The two half loops will equal a full loop, eliminating a weak spot in your pile. All strips begin and end on the top surface of your rug. For this reason, I like to use the longest strips of wool that I can comfortably manage, creating fewer cut ends on top of the pile.

Hide all your cut ends in various places throughout the rug. Avoid having rows of strips start and stop in the same place. Rows of cut ends become unsightly and also weaken that portion of the rug.

Covering the Foundation

You will see some foundation beneath the finished rug unless you are working in fine cuts and skipping just one thread between loops and rows. If you attempt to cover all the foundation, #8 cut becomes very bulky and will not lie flat. Corners and small areas such as leaves cannot be completely filled in. When the rug is flat on the floor, these "empty" spaces will disappear into the body of the work. You never want to see foundation peeking out between loops on top of the rug.

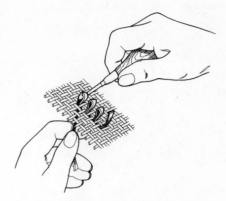

Skip two threads between 1/4-inch-wide loops. This will avoid unsightly packing of your loops, which would prevent your rug from lying flat on the floor.

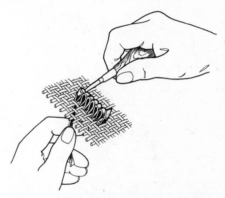

Finer cuts require skipping only one thread between loops when using a primitive foundation material.

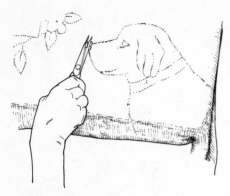

When changing colors, clip off the top of your loop to ensure a clean cut.

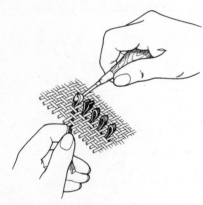

After completing a strip, clip the last loop on top of the work. Begin the next strip in the same hole to prevent a weak spot in your rug.

Hooking Tips

If the strip twists when being drawn up through the mesh, pull it about 1 inch higher than the pile, then retract it from below to 1/4 inch in height. This will straighten out the twist. If your strips are constantly twisting, you may be twisting your hook to pull up the loop. Stop it!

If the strip frays from the action of the hook, you are not releasing the loop properly with your right hand. Before retracting the hook, turn it sideways as though you were pouring water from a cup. When you get in the habit of releasing the hook in this manner, the action will be automatic.

Very fine cuts #3, #4, and #5 may fray when retracting the hook. Lift the loop higher to release the hook, then pull it down to rug level with the left hand under the frame. With tiny strips, turning the hook sideways may make "chenille" of your strand.

Outlining the Motifs

Every object must be outlined with a row of hooking before you fill in the space. This will maintain the shape and give your rows of loops something to bump up against when filling in the area. And then, too, every shape must be outlined by the adjacent color. This will serve the same purpose. When hooking a background, outline not only around the subject, but also around the outside edge. This will keep the rectangle straight and again give a row to hook to and turn from.

Directional Hooking

The direction of hooking is essential to the look of the work. The play of light on loops will enhance the interest of your rug. This texture is created by directional hooking. Straight, typewriterlike rows lend a severity to the pattern. Wavy lines give a playful and gentle feel.

Think of your rug as a coloring book. After outlining, fill in a shape or motif by hooking your rows in the direction that nature would take. When hooking an animal, follow the direction that fur would grow. When filling in flowers and leaves, follow the contour of the shape, going from light to dark or vice versa, depending on the color of the surrounding area. You will have to plan ahead to guarantee a contrast. When hooking a geometric shape, strike a line and keep to it. A curved line is difficult, but following its direction into the center maintains the shape. Hook and fill in spheres in a spiral fashion. Do not cut each row as it joins itself.

Hooking Flowers

My approach to hooking flowers is not realistic. For those of you who enjoy tapestry hooking, you may cut the wool finer and hook your flowers in a lifelike manner. I, however, prefer the watercolor approach rather than the colored pencil rendition. Slightly wider strips (#6 cut) combined with tiny centers (#4 cut) will define the four- to six-shade gradations that produce the flowers in this book. Work in the manner that suits you best.

In all cases, I have noted the size of the cut needed for various parts. This is the widest cut that you may use in order to reproduce the rug as shown. You may always cut narrower strips for even more definition, but wider strips will obliterate the Victorian look and produce a more primitive rug.

Mix your cuts as you would vary the size of your strokes with a paintbrush—larger cut for large areas, smaller cuts for small areas, and tiny cuts for accents.

Filling in the Background

Before you begin hooking, plan the direction of your background rows. Simple subjects can take complicated backgrounds. Involved subject matter fares best with simple backgrounds. A favorite background of mine is wavy rows. Undulating rows are unobtrusive, but not dull.

For contouring backgrounds, follow the contour of the center of interest, and continue to do so in ever-increasing concentric rows, flattening out as they approach the border. These contouring lines will eventually catch up with the several border rows you initially hooked to stabilize the rectangle of the rug.

Using a black permanent marker, draw indications of the background direction on your pattern before you start to hook. I use broken lines to avoid confusion. The area exposed by the frame forbids a view of the whole pattern; drawing these directional lines will give you a well-integrated background flow.

Primitive farm rugs were often hooked in straight typewriterlike rows because of the narrow space visible on homemade sawbuck or quilt type frames. We can lift and shift on lap frames today, allowing more involved and interesting backgrounds.

Don't let your background compete with the subject when using #6 or #8 cut strips. Directional hooking can get very complex if you draw in too many curlicues. The patterns presented in this book keep the backgrounds relatively simple to complement the subject matter. These are informal and casual rugs.

Hooking the Border

To help maintain the rug's rectangular shape, I always hook a row of the border before I begin to fill in the background.

When turning a 90-degree corner, hook two spaces past the last loop before changing direction. These last two sideways loops equal one straight forward loop when the corner is turned. Without this extra loop, the corner will grow soft and rounded. Turn it smartly!

Diagonal hooking in borders is very difficult to keep flat. Diagonal lines distort the rug unless the direction of hooking is reversed in equal amounts. That's why chevrons are popular. If you are using diagonals, to prevent your rug from twisting out of shape, stabilize the rectangle by hooking in the outside two rows before beginning the border design.

I always end a rug with at least two outside border rows of plain hooking. This not only finishes the rug nicely, but also leaves a little extra in case puppy chews on the edge, kitty sharpens her claws, or Dad catches the corner in the door. I've repaired all three.

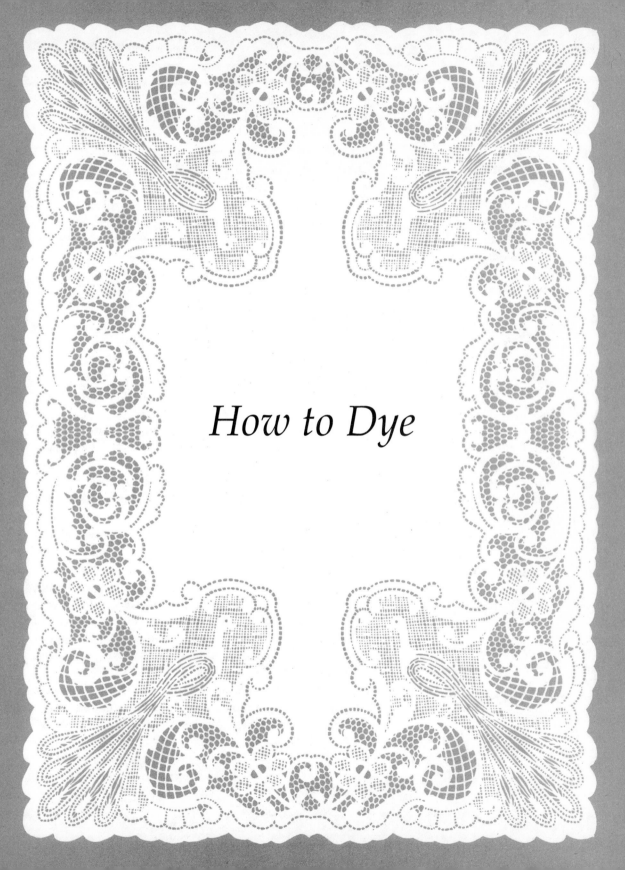

How to Dye

Equipment Needed for Dyeing

*enamel, glass, or stainless steel
    dye pots with lids*

*enamel, glass, or stainless steel
    casserole pan*

*canning kettle or roaster for jar
    dyeing, with lid*

*jars (1-pint or 1-quart) to fit in
    dye vessel*

*dye spoons: TOD or Grey for finer
    gradations)*

Pyrex measuring cups

plain salt (no iodine)

white vinegar

mild detergent

tongs and large heavy fork

paper towels

measuring spoons

aluminum foil

newsprint or newspaper

squirt water bottle

*PROChem WashFast Acid dyes
    and appropriate acid chemi-
    cals*

Cushing dyes

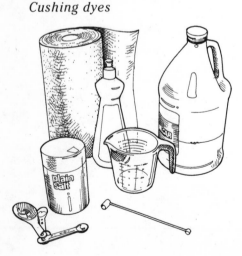

The New Acid Dyes

Cushing Acid Dye Reformulations

In October 1993, the Cushing Dye Company began to reformulate their union Ordinary dyes to acid dyes. These new acid dyes have not been labeled as such and are on the market in the same dye packets as the old union Ordinary dyes. The dyes have been reformulated on the basis of inventory: When a union color runs out, an acid color will replace it. The Cushing Dye Company will furnish a list of the new acid colors on request so that you can know which are union and which are acid at this time. This is necessary because the new acid dyes require a different dyeing process and pose limitations on the old union dyeing techniques.

In order to differentiate the old union and new acid Cushing dyes, you can do several tests:

1. Ask your supplier whether the dyes are union or acid. The packs will look the same, but may be marked with a red line at the top.

2. Open the pack. If the dry dye color looks strangely different from the old familiar Ordinary dye, it is acid.

3. Acid dye will not dye plant fibers. Using a small amount of dye, attempt to dye a piece of white cotton, such as rug tape. If there is no color pickup, the dye is acid.

Because Cushing Dye Company has not completely reformulated all their old union Ordinary dyes at the writing of this book, and I have not completely formulated all my PROChem colors, I include a variety of sources for the colors used in this book. There are many teachers, suppliers, and master dyers, listed in Sources, who can supply your wool needs to make these patterns.

If you have the old Cushing dyes, the colors will be about the same, but the process is different. Use the old Ordinary dye process, which we know and love so well, as described in my first book, *Country Rugs*.

Union dyes may be used to improve and change the

new acid dyes. Because of their rapid takeup, they often even out and improve acid colors. They are compatible and may be mixed with acid dye colors as a corrective measure.

Acid dyes require a high degree of acid pH to absorb the dye into the wool. For Cushing acid dyes, I use vinegar (and it takes lots!). Ammonium sulfate or citric acid may be used with PROChem WashFast Acid dyes. Ammonium sulfate is good to use for pale shades, but add vinegar for additional takeup near the end of the dyeing process for darker colors.

PROChem WashFast Acid Dyes

Frankly, you need an experienced instructor to teach you how to handle PROChem Acid dyes. The metric system, which is daunting to the average home dyer, is used for PROChem dyeing. I have created simple formulas successfully using proportions to make the switch from working with Cushing acid dyes (which are already formulated) to comparable PROChem colors.

PROChem WashFast Acid dyes (see Sources), which are also lightfast, are formulated for silk, wool, and nylon. (I will not discuss silk.) Many wools are woven with some nylon, such as Woolrich plaids (80 percent wool, 20 percent nylon). These fibers both dye beautifully with acid dyes. All PROChem WashFast Acid dye colors intermix well and dye with a minimum of salt and acid. Ammonium sulfate or citric acid is often substituted for vinegar, and a great deal less is used to create the acid pH dye bath.

PROChem WashFast Acid dyes are pure color, with four yellows, five reds, six blues, and a pure black. Several secondary (mix) colors are also available. Keep in mind that you must measure these pure brilliant colors very carefully to achieve pleasant dye shades. There are dye books (see Sources) that will help you mix desired colors. The PROChem dye workshop is very worthwhile as a primary source—almost essential to understand the chemistry of acid dyeing using metric measurements.

Color formulas must be obtained from other sources,

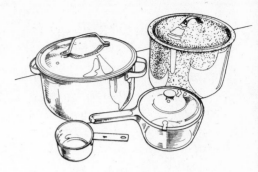

Use only inert dye pots—stainless steel, glass, or enamel. These will not interact with the chemical process and do not absorb dye. A measuring cup holds boiling water to dissolve the dry dye.

Water for Acid Dyeing

Acid dyes are forgiving of city water. Tap water will do the job, except in the summer when the municipal system is loaded with chlorine (smell it!). Our well water is untreated and responds well to acid dyeing using the recommended wetting agent for presoaking and dyeing the wool.

Hard water, full of minerals and metals, can change the shade of the dye, usually dulling it. Acid dyes need soft water for takeup, hence the wetting agents. Do not use detergents to accomplish this goal. Most contain bleach (New! Improved!) and spot the wool during the dyeing process.

Rain and snow in our area are acidic, as in most of the Northeast. Although this soft water dyes my colors beautifully, I was cautioned by experts not to use these waters in the house. Being acidic, these products of the sky will release their toxins when heated. Likewise, distilled water from your dehumidifier can also release condensed gases in your home. I live near Three Mile Island. Enough said.

however. If you cannot take a class, I would suggest simple dyeing with PROChem. WF #672 Jet Black is a pure black with which to overdye bright colors for antique black backgrounds. WF #503 Acid Brown is a perfect khaki drab for dulling bright colors. Used in a weak solution, it is the old khaki drab we once used for bone and pale backgrounds. Half black and half blue make a lovely old Williamsburg blue found in many of the color formulas from master dyers.

Master dyer and teacher Maryanne Lincoln is now transposing her "County Colors" to PROChem dye formulas. She is the best source for learning PROChem dyeing for rug making, as she has adapted metric PROChem to manageable formulas. Her course is tailored to the rug-hooking dyer and completely covers the theory of color, dye formulas, dye techniques, and metric conversions necessary to understand acid dyeing. She is a marvel! I cannot recommend her dye classes too strongly. Her fabric charts, mathematical conversions, and metric breakdowns are astounding to those of us who found math a difficult subject. Maryanne's "Country Colors" are soft, beautiful, and perfect for the rugs shown in this book.

Other master dyers have also devised dye formulas using their choice of primary PROChem dyes to gain a wide range of colors for hooked rugs. Books are available on their color formulations (see Sources).

Acid Dye Precautions

It is hazardous to ignore safety precautions when using acid dyes. Read and strictly observe the manufacturer's instructions. I am indebted to the PRO Chemical and Dye workshop and Don Weiner for helping me with these guidelines.

Never process acid dyes in the microwave if you intend to use this appliance for food. The walls of the microwave remain cool which will condense anything that is volatilized. These particles may then fall back on food prepared in this space. Just as you would not use dye pots for food preparation, do not use your microwave for dyeing purposes, to be on the safe side.

Avoid contact with the skin. Always wear gloves when working with dyes. Heavy lined rubber household gloves are a must for dip dyeing. Surgical gloves can be worn for measuring dye and stirring, as the gloves will not get saturated. Use tongs to move the wool.

Avoid breathing dye powders. Dust and mist face masks are advisable when measuring dry dyes, as tiny particles become airborne and drift when being handled. Measure dry dyes in a still location, not under a ventilating fan.

Cover all surfaces in the dye area with paper towels or other disposable paper dampened with a squirt bottle of water. This will absorb any airborne dye and make it very visible when it lands. When the dyeing session is complete, carefully discard the paper.

Tap the acid dye jar lid smartly before opening it to dislodge any dye from the lid. Use a TOD spoon or Grey measuring spoon, and level the amount with a popsicle stick (disposable) for accurate measurement. Place the measured dye immediately into a cup holding a few drops of hot water. This will dissolve and wet down the dye. Stir the dye into a paste with your popsicle stick, then add 1 cup of boiling water to make the dye solution. Discard the popsicle stick.

Wash all dyeing utensils in a separate sink away from the kitchen. Do not use food utensils as dyeing tools: pots, pans, jars, measuring cups, tongs, or stirring rods. Store dyeing utensils away from the kitchen area so that there is no room for confusion.

Do not smoke, eat, or drink in the dyeing area, and remove food from the vicinity.

Heat the acid dye bath in a well-ventilated area. I always work outside on a card table in the driveway. I use a one-ring burner wired with a waterproof outlet box so that I will not be electrocuted. . . my electrician was concerned. When opening the lid of the simmering dye bath, do so carefully to avoid breathing in the acid fumes.

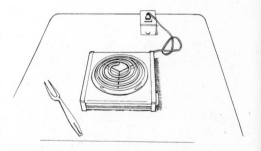

Work in a well-ventilated area when using acid dyes. I use a card table and an electric burner with a waterproof outlet set up outside in my driveway.

Cool dye in the dye pots so that when you empty the pot, the acid fumes are not active. Wipe up all dye spills immediately with paper towels so that the dried dye particles will not drift. Thoroughly clean up the stove, sink, and dye area with detergent on disposable paper towels. Rinse and dry with disposable towels. Do not use kitchen dishcloths or towels. Vacuum the area when dyeing is completed. Do not sweep.

Store all well-labeled acid dye chemicals, utensils, and dye pots out of the reach of children and pets, and far from the kitchen area.

The Acid Dyeing Process

The method of dyeing with acid dyes is different than with union dyes. Mottled dyeing—throwing wool into a dye pot, stirring once, then leaving it to absorb color in an uneven fashion—can no longer be accomplished the same way. Graduated strip dyeing and dip dyeing also must be done with new procedures. As my patterns do not call for multicolored or violent changes in color, these new procedures must be adhered to in order to obtain the effects as pictured. Acid dyes take up at different rates for each color in the formulation (for example, using green dye, blue will absorb first and yellow last). For this reason, to attain success, learning the new acid dye process is mandatory.

Prewetting the Wool
Acid dyes will take up more readily in soft water. Be sure to presoak your wool in Synthrapol (PROChem) or Wetter than Water (available from Ramona Maddox). These lower the surface tension of the water, allowing the wool to wet-out faster; they are available from your supplier (see Sources). Detergent, because it usually contains a bleach, does not do the job. Add a few drops or a squirt of wetting agent, depending on the hardness of your water, to the presoaking water. A slight foam will result, and the wool will sink. White wool takes about 1/2 hour. Nat-

ural unbleached wool takes a great deal longer to soak through completely. Allow it to soak overnight. Use this "wetting" water to add to your dye bath to further soften the dye water, and do not rinse or wring out the "water wetter" from your wool before dyeing.

Making the Dye Solution

Be sure to read carefully the "Precautions for Acid Dyes" earlier in this chapter. Acid dye is not to be used carelessly.

Measure the dye with a dye spoon. Use a popsicle stick to even off the dye so the amount is exact. Dissolve the measured dye amount into a few drops of hot water in a Pyrex measuring cup. Stir to make a paste before adding 1 cup of boiling water to completely dissolve the dye.

PROChem dyes are stronger colors than Cushing acid dyes and require smaller amounts of dye. For these dyes, and Cushing dyes as well, use TOD spoons ($1/32$ teaspoon and $1/4$ teaspoon) or Grey dye spoons ($1/128$ to 1 teaspoon).

In general, remember that $1/32$ teaspoon of Cushing dye will produce a medium shade on 1 ounce of wool for that dye color. Determine how dark you wish your darkest value to be in dyeing graduated strips. I use $3/32$ teaspoon of Cushing acid dye to be sure that I have enough dye solution for the darkest value when dyeing in jars or open pans. The proportion of dye to wool, salt, and acid will be the same regardless of the method of dyeing.

Applying the Heat

Acid dyeing begins with all the ingredients at room temperature. Dissolve the dye in 1 cup of boiling water, then add cool water to reduce the heat of the solution. Dissolve salt and a PROChem acid (if using PROChem dye) in warm water, then add to the dye bath. Prewetted wool will also be at room temperature. Adding the acid and gradually applying heat will begin the dye process. For this reason, it is necessary to thoroughly saturate the wool with the tepid dye bath to dye evenly and avoid unwanted splotches.

All wool must be processed for one hour from the beginning of the simmer stage for the desired color. Shades of light to dark cannot be dyed in the same dye pot as previously done with union dyes, as the components enter the wool at different stages. To achieve various shades, wool must be dyed individually in separate containers using various proportions of the dye solution. For this reason, jar dyeing and open pan dyeing are the preferred methods of achieving shades with small amounts of wool.

Adding the Acid

In addition to gradual heating, acid dyes need vinegar (or another acid) for dye takeup. I use 5% white distilled (cooking) vinegar to process Cushing acid dyes. It takes a great deal more than the old union dye bath. I will henceforth refer to the acid additive as vinegar. For PROChem dyes, I use a PROChem acid. Plain salt (no iodine) is added as a leveler to both types of acid dyes. It does not prevent or assist in takeup, but it evens out the color on the wool. It must be added before the wool is immersed in the dye bath.

Vinegar is the vital ingredient for takeup. One to 2 cups per yard may be needed, particularly with dark colors and those with a lot of yellow (which needs high heat as well).

Regardless of what dye companies may tell you, do not add the vinegar to begin the dye bath. Add it after ten to fifteen minutes of gradual heating. Divide the vinegar quantity in half or quarters and add every ten to fifteen minutes of the dyeing process to assist in takeup. Adding vinegar in large quantities to the original tepid dye bath or to a hot dye bath causes massive splotching of the wool, generally in the blue range. Adding vinegar a little at a time controls the dye takeup, as acid dye will absorb only in the presence of acid and heat.

Working the Wool

The third component for successful acid takeup is frequent motion or working the wool. This is necessary so that the various color components will attach themselves evenly to the wool fibers. If you do not move the dye bath every five minutes, the wool will be covered with unwanted spots. To work the wool, whether in an open pan or a jar, move the stirring rod sideways across the dye pot, first in one direction, then the other. This crosswise movement will open the wool for a more even acceptance of the dye. Stirring round and round does not accomplish this goal, but twists the wool together. Working the wool becomes critical when the dye bath begins to heat. As the temperature rises, the dye begins to grab in the presence of acid. At this point, stir constantly for very even dyeing results.

When the wool has totally absorbed the dye, the process is complete. Permit the wool to cool in the dye pot.

Washing and Drying the Wool

After the dyed wool has cooled in the dye pot, spin it out in the washer. If you do not intend to spot dye or further process your wool, add a drop of mild detergent and wash the wool gently in lukewarm, not cold, water. Rinse thoroughly and do not agitate. I turn off the agitation on the wash and rinse cycles to prevent matting. Sudden changes of temperature or agitation will shrink your wool.

Spin out the rinse water, and dry the wool in the dryer until it is fluffy, but still damp. Do not use a fabric softener sheet. This deposits a film on the wool that will make cutting the strips sticky and difficult. Finish drying the wool completely on a rack, shower rod, or ironing board so that it does not distort or wrinkle. Do not iron the strips. You want them to be soft and bouncy.

Acid Dye Directions

Open Pan Dyeing

For open pan dyeing, first dissolve the dye in a 1-cup measure with several drops of hot water to make a paste. Then completely dissolve this paste with 1 cup of

Dyeing with Kool-Aid

As all "sheep to shawl" spinners and weavers, kindergarten teachers, and mothers of small children know, Kool-Aid is a dye! This dye technique is on par with using chocolate pudding for fingerpaint. Nevertheless, both work!

Using various colors, and this is strictly experimental, Kool-Aid can tint white wool or overdye unwanted colors. A rug student of mine (thanks, Caroline!) showed me her dye chart of overdyed bright and unusable colors that had been softened, dulled, and splotched with Kool-Aid. Amazing! Grape flavor can mottle and dramatically change vivid yellow-greens or tone down fire-engine red. I like the look and the process. It is safe, easy, and carefree. Merely presoak the wool, no vinegar or salt required, place it in a pan or crockpot, simmer for about one hour, and the miracle occurs.

boiling water. Add the designated amount of salt to a
room temperature dye pot half full of water. If using
PROChem dyes, add ammonium sulfate to the water at
this time. Stir the additives to dissolve them, and add
the dye solution. Stir thoroughly to completely incorpo-
rate the chemicals. Use lots of water, as the wool must
move easily through the dye bath to take up evenly. Add
the soaking water to soften the water in the dye bath.
Add the presoaked wool wetted by a wetting agent. Carefully lift and lower the wool in the open pan to saturate
the entire piece. You must work the wool, pushing it
sideways back and forth, to fully saturate all surfaces to
ensure that the dye has penetrated the wool before
adding heat and acid.

With Cushing acid dyes, vinegar will be used as an
acid. With PROChem WashFast, acid (ammonium sulfate) has already been added to the dye bath. Turn on
the heat, gradually raising the temperature and stirring
the wool every five minutes. As the temperature rises,
after fifteen minutes, and before the simmer stage, add
the designated amount of vinegar. Lift the wool, add the
premeasured vinegar, stir, and lower the wool into the
dye bath. Acid dyes must be worked often and thoroughly to allow the full spectrum of dye components to
enter the fabric at their allotted times in the dyeing
process. The original color of the wool will change as
each component enters the fabric. For this reason, wool
cannot be added or removed during the process, as it
will lack some of the necessary dye ingredients.

Remember that blue enters first and yellow last, so
don't panic but keep on heating and stirring. From the
time of simmer, the acid dye process takes one hour to
mature. Leave the wool cool in the dye pot for final
takeup.

Large pieces of wool, such as background wool, must
have acid added by thirds or fourths to ensure unspot-
ted wool. A large quantity of acid to begin will grab in
hot spots at the bottom of your pan, leaving unsightly
splotches (generally blue) on your wool. I lift and lower
the larger pieces, adding vinegar as the heat rises to
assist in gradual takeup. You will see the dye bath

beginning to clear. Don't stop working the wool. Add the final amount of vinegar when the water seems clear—it isn't. If, after sixty minutes, the dye still hasn't taken up, dump in more vinegar. Dark colors need more acid than light shades.

In addition, yellow needs high heat to complete the takeup. If the dye bath is not clear, turn up the heat after one hour of the above, bringing the dye bath to a rapid boil, stir, and simmer ten more minutes. Keep the lid on and turn off the heat, permitting the wool to cool in the dye bath.

Depending on the value of the color, you may not have to simmer the wool for a full hour. When the color is absorbed, the dye action is complete, but allow the wool to cool in the dye bath for true color results. Then wash, rinse, and dry the wool.

Jar Dyeing

Jar dyeing takes one hour to process in 1-pint jars and one and a half hours to process in 1-quart jars.

Most jar dyeing is done with six to eight jars for a great range of shades. Because you are using #6 cut (mostly) for the designs in this book, four or five gradations of color will be sufficient.

Using the dye formulas for each chapter, you will need pint or quart jars depending on the quantity of wool needed for each color. Use wide-mouth jars such as canning, peanut butter, or mayonnaise jars. Remember that you can never again use these jars for food. Thin, cracked, or narrow-mouthed jars are unacceptable.

If you plan to dye small amounts (3-by-12-inch to 3-by-24-inch strips), use 1-pint jars. Large amounts up to 9 by 24 inches can be dyed in 1-quart jars. A lot of water is necessary to move the wool to prevent unwanted splotching. Do not pack the wool strips in the jars; this would prevent them from receiving equal access to the dye bath.

Presoaking the Wool

Presoak the wool in the chosen wetting agent. Use a squirt or two, depending on the quantity of the wool and

Small swatches of wool can be dyed by the jar method. This is a favorite method of dyeing graduated strips of color.

the hardness of your water. Agitate the wetting agent in warm water before adding the wool. Use a sink, a kettle, or the washer. Soak white wool for one hour, natural wool overnight. The wool will sink when it is saturated.

Preparing the Dye Solution

Be sure to read carefully the "Precautions for Acid Dyes" earlier in this chapter before opening the dye. Acid dyes are not the casual union dyes you have been using in the past. Work in a draftfree area, wear gloves and a mask, and cover the dye area with damp newspaper or damp paper towels. Acid dye is airborne and must not be inhaled.

At the bottom of a calibrated Pyrex measuring cup, add several drops of hot water before adding the dry dye. Make a paste, stirring well to break up the beads of dye. Now add 1 cup of boiling water to completely dissolve the dye paste. Stir the dye solution.

Add 1/2 teaspoon of salt to each 1-pint jar or 1 teaspoon per quart jar. Pour half of the dissolved dye solution into jar one. Add water to refill the measuring cup to 1 cup, and pour half of this solution into jar two. Repeat this procedure for as many jars as you need shades. You will end up with 1/2 cup of unused pale dye solution. If the last solution is very pale, you can add the remaining 1/2 cup to the last jar; otherwise, discard it. Stir these jar solutions, and add wetting water to half the capacity of the jar.

Adding the Wool

Accordion pleat large pieces to add to the jars. Small strips can be lowered and raised with tongs. Squeeze out the wool strips—do not rinse—and lower the wool gently into the jars. Thoroughly saturate the strips by working the wool—sideways in the case of large pieces, lifting and lowering with small strips. The jars will be filled near the top with wool and the dye bath. Add more water if needed, but leave room for 2 tablespoons of vinegar to be added later. Do not cover the individual jars.

Heating the Wool

Place the jars in your canning vessel or dye pot. Pour in warm tap water to three-fourths the height of the jars. Begin to heat the vessel on low heat. The heat must rise slowly. Continue to heat with the lid on, stirring the wool every five minutes. Lift and lower small strips; work the larger pieces. After fifteen minutes of heating, pour 1 tablespoon of vinegar into each jar. Premeasure the vinegar to begin with so that adding 1 tablespoon at a time doesn't require four hands.

Lift out the wool before adding the vinegar, stir, and return. Continue working the wool as the heat rises. Add another tablespoon of vinegar in another fifteen minutes. The wool should be simmering. Now is the critical time for dye takeup. Permit the wool to simmer (lid on), stirring often, for one hour. Deep colors may take longer and need more vinegar. When the dye bath is clear, remove the jars and cool in the dye bath. Continue heating uncleared dye bath jars until takeup is complete. Yellow will need higher heat and possibly more vinegar.

Wool with a heavy load of dye that does not entirely clear the dye bath must be set separately in a pan of clean water with a splash of vinegar. Simmer to a boil, turn off the heat, and cool in the pan.

Dip Dyeing

To dip dye the acid way, dissolve the dye as in the general directions according to your formula. Place one-fourth of the dye solution in a large quantity of warm water in the dye pot. Add 1 teaspoon of plain salt and 1/4 cup of vinegar, and stir. Lay the entire piece of wool to be dip dyed into this weak dye bath, opening, stirring, and simmering the wool until the dye bath is clear.

Wearing heavy-lined rubber gloves, lift the wool out of the dye bath and add another one-fourth of the dye solution, 1/4 cup of vinegar, and 1 teaspoon of salt to the dye bath. Stir thoroughly, and reimmerse the wool into the dye bath, dipping and dunking three-fourths (or however many sections of color you desire) of the pale

Dip dyeing is done in a sequential fashion. Adding dye in stages and lifting and lowering the wool until takeup will produce a large piece with the color flowing from light to dark.

When dip dyeing, add dye in graduated stages, resting the previously dyed piece in an adjacent pan. Stir the new dye solution with additional salt and vinegar before reimmersing the wool for a deeper shade.

Dip dyeing with acid dye takes a long time. You can rest your arm by slumping the wool in a corner of the pan or removing it to an adjacent basin before adding more dye.

wool. Continue simmering, dipping, and dunking the wool to the correct level. Do this casually until the dye bath is cleared once more, as you do not want a defined demarcation line.

Repeat the process, adding more dye solution, salt, and vinegar, dipping and dunking, until each quarter of the wool is dyed and the dye bath is clear. This will tell you that the dye has matured. The first immersion will produce the lightest shade and the last addition of dye will give you the darkest shade. Simmer the entire piece for ten more minutes, and leave it to cool in the pan. If your arm gets tired holding the wool, dipping and dunking, place an auxiliary pan beside the dye pot, and drape the previously dyed wool over the edge into the holding pan. This may drip on your stove, but you need a break.

Painted Dyeing

Previously dyed wool can be overdyed by painting the wool with a paintbrush or rubbing the dye in with the back of a spoon. This is a terrific effect for shaded leaves.

Painting Green Leaves

If you have just dyed your wool with Cushing Reseda Green, do not rinse the wool after completing the dying process. If using purchased material, presoak the wool, then dip it in a solution of half water and half vinegar. Squeeze out the excess liquid.

In separate wide-mouthed measuring cups, make one solution of $1/32$ teaspoon Yellow and another of $1/64$ teaspoon Dark Green using Cushing dyes in 1 cup of boiling water each. Tear the wool strips into the appropriate lengths that will accommodate the length of your hooked leaf. I find this out by hooking one row at the outside edge, ripping it out, and then measuring it for length. This measurement will permit uniform shading from front to back of the leaf. Be generous; the excess you clip off can be used for flower centers.

Lay out the strips, lasagna style, in a foil-lined enamel casserole pan, sprinkle on some salt, and brush on the dark green dye solution from one end and the yellow dye solution from the other end toward the middle, leaving the center third unpainted. Use a separate brush for each color.

If the length of wool needed for the leaf is longer than the pan, push up the excess wool into the unpainted center of the strip. Work the dye into the wool, gradually lifting the brush as it approaches the center. The ends will be the darkest shades.

Lay one layer on top of the other, adding a sprinkling of salt to each layer. Add a small amount of vinegar water, if needed. The water level cannot be too great or the dyes will run together, ruining your three-tone effect. Cover the casserole with aluminum foil and steam for one hour. Check to be sure that the pan does not run dry. Add more vinegar water in tiny drips to the wool if the pan looks dry. Cool, wash, and rinse.

You can use a paintbrush to add different dye solutions to the wool swatch. Brushing dye from each end into the center will produce a variegated piece, especially nice for leaves.

Transitional Dyeing

Using the painted dyeing technique, brush from one color to another over the entire length of a white pre-soaked strip. Stick to a related color family. Complements (opposites on the color wheel) will create a muddy color if they overlap in the center. I have created lovely fall leaves in this manner, brushing bright rust to brown, and for an antique sky, brushing from pale gold to light blue. The possibilities are endless. Experiment!

Spot Dyeing

Wools that have been previously dyed can be spot dyed with acid dyes in the same manner that we used for union dyes. Mottling the wool is no longer possible with acid dyes, but wool can be further spot dyed after the initial process, using open pan dyeing, to achieve a similar effect.

To spot dye, use a very weak dye solution of your original formula. Squeeze out the wool and then return it to the pan, leaving all the dye chemicals (salt, acid, and prewetting agent) still in the drippy wool. Arrange the wool in crowded folds, and drip dots of the weak dye on top of the wool. This top area will need an additional

Spot dyeing with acid dyes may be accompanied by scrunching previously dyed wool into a dye pot and adding small spots of diluted dye solution to the top of the crowded folds.

thirty minutes to set and mature the dye spots. Keep these areas light! If the dye spots look too dark, dilute them with some warm water.

For larger background pieces, add a very weak original dye solution plus 1/4 cup of vinegar to the bottom of the dye pot, about 1 inch deep. Crowd your wool as directed above, and push it down into the weak dye bath. Now use more of this diluted dye on top of the crowded folds as described above. These two techniques will spot both the top and bottom of the wool in an uneven manner to give the background area a mottled effect. Process the dye as above.

Another method of achieving a mottled look is to start with wools of various shades of white. Dyeing white, natural wool, and a very light bone together in the same dye pot will produce different shades of a color that can be cut and mixed when hooking in the area. This is effective if the colors are very close in value and hooked alternately into the background.

Casserole Dyeing

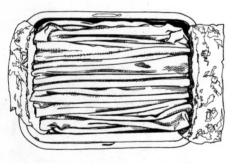

For casserole dyeing, accordion fold a piece of wool in an oblong pan.

Fold presoaked, predyed wool in accordion pleats in a foil-lined casserole pan. Using several pale dye solutions, with 1 teaspoon of salt and 1/4 cup of vinegar each, dribble on the colors in alternate rows, leaving some of the wool free of dye. This will produce a diffused and mottled effect. Remember to pour the dye solutions against the selvage for a mottled strip. Pouring on dye with the selvage will produce rows of color when you cut the wool.

Dyeing with Onion Skins

Several of the patterns in my book use onion skin dyes. Refer to "Rousseau's Tiger" and "Corgi" for instructions on dyeing with onion skins, and to "Beehive" for spotting with onion skins.

Troubleshooting

If your dyed wool has a white core visible when cut, more wetting agent is needed in the presoak or the wool

needs overnight soaking. Vinegar and heat should be
added more gradually to the dye bath.

If the heat is too high, the wool takes up too rapidly
and will become splotchy from the various colors con-
tained in the dye. To avoid this problem, apply heat
more slowly and stir more frequently.

Some acid dyes are not compatible with each other.
For example, acid Khaki Drab does not mix well with
other colors and deposits dirty-looking spots on the wool.

Yellows need more heat and acid for takeup. Add
both, if your dye bath is still yellow after one hour of
simmering.

If your arm gets tired or you get distracted when processing wool for one hour, well, snap out of it! This is
what acid dyeing takes. Keep on stirring! If the phone
rings or your arm needs a rest, keep an auxiliary pan
adjacent to the dye pot. Flop the wool into it, and then
reimmerse when you can continue working the wool. If
jar dyeing is interrupted, turn off the heat and remove
the jars from the dye pot, and pray that the batch is not
ruined. Acid dyeing takes time and effort!

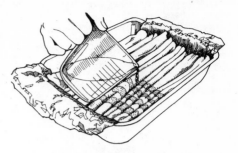

*Pour pale dye solutions in alter-
nate rows to produce a diffused
and mottled piece of wool. This
is a nice effect for dyeing a sky.*

Home Sweet Home

In the wake of the Civil War, the political slogan "Peace and Plenty" reflected the desire for personal comfort after the devastation of war. To symbolize this dream, design motifs were drawn from other ages. The cornucopia, ancient symbol of bountiful harvest, spilling fruit and flowers, or urns spilling more of the same were popular signs of abundance.

Victorians loved ornamentation. No surface was left empty, and knick-knacks of all kinds were collected and displayed. Possessions indicated prosperity. Modern conveniences and the funds to hire help gave housewives the time to do handicrafts. These handicrafts were not only fashionable, but reflected the gentility of the woman's use of leisure time, an outward sign of the breadwinner's financial success.

A man's home was his castle, and the rise in work away from the home, as opposed to the farm community, turned the home from the workplace into a retreat at the day's end. The housewife, freed from the drudgery of farm work, spent hours making the home cozy. Hooking rugs was part of that effort.

PATTERN

"Home Sweet Home"

22½ by 42 inches

MATERIALS

Using 12-ounce wool per yard, purchase 4 yards of white wool to dye as below.

Cornucopias
2 ounces of medium brown wool (1/6 yard or an 18-by-24-inch sheet).

Basket outlines
1 1/2 ounce or 9-by-24-inch sheet of dark medium wool.

Lettering, red roses, and border
6 ounces (1/2 yard) of medium red wool.

Background
24 ounces (2 yards) of cream wool.

Pink roses
5 shades of pink wool, 1/2 ounce (3 by 24 inches) each.

Dark red roses and buds
1 ounce (6-by-24-inch sheet) dark red wool.

Gold flowers
3 shades of gold wool, 1/2 ounce (3 by 24 inches) each.

Blue flowers
Scraps of blue wool: 1/2 ounce light blue, 1/2 ounce medium blue (3 by 24 inches each).

Leaves
4 ounces for 8 shades of green wool (1/2 ounce each) *or* 4-value swatch of four 3-by-24-inch strips each of Dark Green, Reseda Green, and Myrtle Green.

Veins
Scraps of overdyed dark green plaid. Scraps of overdyed light green plaid.

Flower centers
Scraps of bright gold wool.

DYES
(Cushing Perfection Acid Dye)

Old Gold

Golden Brown

Medium Brown

Egyptian Red

Reseda Green

Dark Green

Myrtle Green

Copenhagen Blue (if needed)

Berlin Work

The popular song "Home Sweet Home" typified the sentimental tastes of Victorians in all spheres of life who
framed the song's words in Berlin work and cross-stitch
samplers on parlor walls. Sentimental and religious sayings, such as "Welcome Friends," "God Is Love," and
"Bless This House," expressed the Victorian reverence
for hearth and home.

These homilies, stitched on punch paper, were
called Berlin work, which got its name from the source
of the woolen yarns dyed in Germany with the new vivid
aniline dyes. The Victorian technology that could perfo-
rate card paper provided a shortcut to the time-consuming counted cross-stitch or needlepoint on canvas that
previously provided an outlet for the needlewoman.

This was pick-up work, as no self-respecting gentle-
woman would have idle hands. From bookmarks to pictures, Berlin work designs were advertised widely in
women's magazines and readily available to middle-
class women (and children), who could choose a motto
most appropriate to their mindset, much like the
needlepoint pillows we modern Victorians display on
our sofas, advising others of our hobbies, opinions, and
foibles.

Tearing the Wool

All the lettering, flowers, leaves, and cornucopias are
cut with #6 cut, and the background and two border
rows are cut with #8. Tear the wool with the selvage for
the #6 cuts.

Plan to tear 1^1/$_3$ yards of white wool into two sections 24 inches long from selvage to selvage. This will
give you two sheets to tear with the selvage into 3-by-24-
inch (or wider) strips for the #6 cut called for in this pattern. Read the directions in chapter 2, under "Tearing
the Wool," before tearing all the strips into 3-inch
widths. Some are left in bigger sheets for ease in dyeing.

Dyeing for "Home Sweet Home"

Dyeing the Cornucopias

To dye the cornucopias, tear a sheet of white wool 18 by 24 inches. I like to use open pan dyeing for this size sheet (see chapter 6). Dissolve $1/32$ teaspoon Medium Brown and $1/32$ teaspoon Golden Brown to make the dye solution, and add 1 teaspoon of salt. Add $1/2$ cup of vinegar in two stages to the dye bath as described in chapter 6.

The darker brown basket dividers (9-by-24-inch sheet) will be dyed in the same open pan dyeing method with $2/32$ teaspoon Medium Brown dye. Use this shade to hook the branches as well.

Dyeing the Lettering, Red Roses, and Border

Presoak $1/2$ yard of white wool or an 18-inch strip. This wool will be dyed in one piece and cut with the selvage. Using the open pan dyeing method, dissolve $1/4$ teaspoon Egyptian Red and 2 teaspoons of salt in 1 cup of boiling water, and add it to a 2-gallon dye pot. Process with open pan dyeing, adding $1/4$ cup of vinegar before the simmer and $1/4$ cup more when the simmer begins. Egyptian Red is a slow takeup. Add extra vinegar near the end of the dye cycle if the dye bath is not exhausted.

Dyeing the Background

Two yards of wool is a lot to process for a 2-gallon dye pot. Unless you have a larger vessel, tear the background wool in half and dye the wool in two different lots, dividing the dye solution and using half in each dye pot.

Prepare the dye solution: $1/32$ teaspoon Old Gold for 2 yards of white wool with 2 teaspoons of salt. Add $1/4$ cup of vinegar at the simmer stage, after thoroughly saturating the wool with the dye, lifting and lowering the wool in the dye bath. Add $1/4$ cup (or more) of vinegar after processing forty-five minutes to exhaust the dye bath. Permit the wool to cool in the dye bath.

Dyeing the Pink Roses

Using graduated strip jar dyeing, tear five strips of white wool into 3-by-24-inch strips. Dissolve $2/32$ teaspoon Egyptian Red for the dye solution in 1 cup of boiling water, plus 1 teaspoon of salt in each jar, and process the strips as directed in chapter 6.

Dyeing the Dark Red Roses and Buds
Presoak a 6-by-24-inch sheet. Dissolve 3/32 teaspoon Egyptian Red with 1 teaspoon of salt in a 1-gallon dye pot. Using the open pan dyeing method, dye the sheet, adding 1/2 cup of vinegar in three stages.

Dyeing the Gold Flowers
For gold roses, you will need three shades in 3-by-24-inch strips of gold plus some of the basket medium brown and some of the background cream. Dissolve 1/64 teaspoon Old Gold and 1/2 teaspoon of salt. Using the jar dyeing process, dye the three strips in three jars. The dark gold shade will be used to top the cornucopias.

Dyeing the Blue Flowers
If light and medium blue scraps are not available, pan dye two 3-by-24-inch strips. Dissolve 1/64 teaspoon Copenhagen Blue in 1 cup of boiling water, and add 1/2 teaspoon of salt. Use half the dye solution in one pan for the medium blue. Refill to 1 cup of water and use 1/2 cup dye solution for the lighter blue strip. Process as above, adding 1/4 cup of vinegar to each container.

Dyeing the Leaves
Because the leaves overlap, a great variety of greens are needed. I used four values of Dark Green, Reseda Green, and Myrtle Green. Tear four 3-by-24-inch strips of white wool for a four-value swatch of each color. Prepare dye solutions of 1/32 teaspoon Dark Green for one series, 1/32 teaspoon Reseda Green for another series, and 1/32 teaspoon Myrtle Green for the third series. The four values of each color will be dyed by the jar method.

Dyeing the Veins
If you have light and dark green plaid scraps (about 3-by-12-inch pieces each) for the leaf veins, plan to dye them with the leaves in separate jars. Make a 1/64 teaspoon

dye solution with Dark Green for green plaid veins and
1/128 teaspoon dye solution of Reseda Green for overdyeing
a light plaid. These jars will be processed in the same
dyeing vessels that you use to process the leaves.

Hooking "Home Sweet Home"

Hooking the Lettering
Using #6 cut, hook the lettering inside the outlines.
Outline one or two rows of background material around
the letters as you go, hooking in the closed areas. Join
the lettering with several rows of undulating hooking,
but be sure not to box in this center, as you want it to
flow into the rest of the background.

Hooking the Cornucopias
Outline the baskets with one row of dark medium
brown (#6 cut). Using medium golden brown (from the
flowers), hook two rows at the top of the baskets. Complete the cornucopias with medium brown wool.

Hooking the Red Roses
Hook the very darkest vein green surrounded by light
gold in the red rose centers. I used three shades of red
for these roses: lettering red, deep red, and the darkest
shade of pink. Use dark red for the buds.

Hooking the Pink Roses
For the pink rose centers, hook vein green surrounded by
pale green. To the five pink shades, add lettering red to
separate the two rings of petals with a darker shadow.

Hooking the Gold Flowers
Hook the centers of the gold flowers with deep red surrounded by one row of background cream. Alternate
light, medium, and dark gold as you hook the flowers,
making sure that a dark or medium shade touches the
cream background so that the flowers do not disappear.
Add "shadows" of basket brown to the gold rose to divide
the inner petals from the outer petals. A strong contrast
is needed with these light values.

Hooking the Blue Flowers

Hook a tiny red spot in the blue flower center surrounded by deep gold. Outline the petals and center in light blue, and fill in with medium blue.

Hooking the Leaves

Plan to use your darkest greens above the cornucopias and framing the bottom center red rose. Alternate shades of light and dark greens, using various veins— light veins on dark leaves, dark veins on medium leaves. The lightest green is used for the bud stamens and sepals, the vine stems, and the palest small leaves. Light Myrtle Green leaves (really an aqua) should be hooked midway between the blue flowers, in the vines (along with other light shades), and mixed in with the other warmer leaves to break up the mass of green. Alternate shades of warm greens so that the leaf shades remain distinct. Hook the stems at the top with medium brown.

Hooking the Background

Place your initials and the date in the bottom corners with medium gold. They should not compete with the red lettering. Now outline all the leaves and flowers with background cream. Continue contour hooking throughout the center of the rug. Contour the hooking around the outside leaves and roses until you straighten out the rows around the outside edges. To keep the rug perfectly straight, hook the red border rows first, before filling in to the outer edges. Two rows of background cream hooked beside these red rows will stabilize the edges as you fill in the background to the border.

Finishing the Rug

I used a macramé fringe to finish the ends of "Home Sweet Home." This fringe can be added while you are binding with yarn. See chapter 11 for instructions on adding fringe.

PATTERN

"Beehive"

30 by 37 inches

DYES
(Cushing's Perfection Acid Dye)

Mummy Brown or natural onion skin dye	Rose
Copenhagen Blue	Maroon
Robin's Egg Blue	Purple
Yellow	Myrtle Green
Ecru	Green
Old Gold	Bronze Green
Egyptian Red	Rust (if needed)

MATERIALS

Maryanne Lincoln will provide your wool needs with the colors suggested below if you do not care to dye for "Beehive" (see Sources).

Bees
 Body. Scraps of 2 shades of brown wool (brown and dark brown).
 Wings and checked veins. Scraps of white and off-white wool.
 Head, legs, and antennae. Scraps of black wool.

Bee skep
 6 ounces (1/2 yard) of camel or oatmeal wool speckled with onion skin.
 Dividers. 1 ounce of overdyed wool or "Sand N3-8, Maryanne Lincoln, Value #3 for the light skep and Value #5 for the dark dividers.
 Entry. Scrap of black wool.

Sky
 6 ounces of French blue wool or 1/2 yard of (Value #2) Country Blue, Maryanne Lincoln.

Trellis
 8 ounces of light bone wool or (Value #4) Magnolia #2, Maryanne Lincoln.

Border background
 10 ounces of black wool.

Rose and poppy
 3-by-12-inch piece for each of the 6 shades of Egyptian Red or one 6-value swatch of Red Poppy, Maryanne Lincoln.

Dogwood
 1/4 ounce of white wool.
 Outlines of petals and centers. Pink and light yellow-green wool scraps from other swatches.
 Flower centers. Scraps of bright gold.
 Branch. Scraps of light camel and medium brown.

Pansy Eyes
 Scraps of black.
 Center. Scraps of yellow-green. 3-by-12-inch piece for each of the 6 shades of light to dark red-purple wool or one 6-value swatch of Light Plum, Maryanne Lincoln.

Trumpet flower
 3-by-12-inch piece for each of the 6 shades of bright pink wool or one 6-value swatch of Lipstick Red, Maryanne Lincoln.

Zinnia and daffodil
 3-by-12-inch piece for each of the 8 shades of gold or one 8-value swatch of Goldenrod, Maryanne Lincoln.

 Daffodil's throat. Scraps of dark and light Tiger Lily, Maryanne Lincoln
 Flower Centers. Scraps of bright yellow-green.

Calla lily and apple blossoms
 1/4 ounce of white wool. Scraps of off-white and light beige wool or one 8-value swatch of Magnolia #2, Maryanne Lincoln.
 Apple blossom stems. Scrap of brown.
 Apple blossom centers. Scrap of deep gold.

Petunia and iris
 3-by-12-inch piece for each of the 6 shades of light to dark purple wool or one 6-value swatch of Atlanta Azalea, Maryanne Lincoln.
 Details. Scrap of gold wool.

Tiger lily
 3-by-12-inch piece for each of the 4 shades of light to golden rust wool or one 6-value swatch of Tiger Lily, Maryanne Lincoln.
 Stamens. Scraps of green wool.
 Pistils. Scraps of maroon wool.

Magnolia
 3-by-12-inch piece for each of the 6 shades of light to dark maroon wool or one 8-value swatch of Magnolia #1, Maryanne Lincoln.
 Branch. Scrap of brown wool.

Daisies
 1/4 ounce of white wool. Scraps of off-white wool or use remaining wool from Magnolia #2.
 Center. Scrap of deep gold.

Leaf greens
 5 ounces of white wool for dyeing three 6-value green groups (blue-green, warm green, yellow-green) or one 6-value swatch of Forest Green, one 6-value swatch of Charcoal Jade (skip the two darkest values), and one 6-value swatch of Moss Green, Maryanne Lincoln.

Victorian Gardens

Nothing says "Victorian" more than flowers, and no cottage was complete without a flower garden. Flower gardens, encouraged by the books of Andrew Jackson Downing, surrounded the country cottage. Blooming beside the kitchen garden, flower beds were often decorated by sundials, trellises, and bee skeps, which had the added advantage of producing honey.

The bee skep, woven of dried grasses, was a garden fixture. With their home centered in a bed of flowers, the bees did not have far to go to gather nectar (or cross-pollinate), and the garden was made sweeter by its presence.

Flowers provided a special outlet for Victorian reticence. The "language of flowers" sent coded messages unfamiliar to us today. Red roses announced true love of a passionate nature. Dogwood suggested durability. The pansy declared thoughts and the trumpet flower fame. Zinnias brought "thoughts of you" and the petunia said, "Never despair." The red poppy offered consolation, but the tiger lily demanded, "Make me proud." Apple blossoms indicated preference, the magnolia dignity. Yellow daffodils signaled regard and iris sent a message, both rather lukewarm sentiments. White daisies and the lily symbolized purity. You can understand that bouquets were not sent without great forethought.

Dyeing for "Beehive"

The beauty of "Beehive" is dependent on the rich, jewel-like colors of the flowers and leaves. By this I do not mean bright and gaudy, but deep vivid shades resonating against the black background. Five to six shades of each color are achieved with graduated strip dyeing. The variety comes from shades of color and repetition in different combinations.

Analyze the color pattern: The reds are in opposite corners (rose and poppy), as are the yellows (zinnia and daffodil); the whites are scattered every fourth block; the purples form a triangle of color; the pinks are diagonal to each other; and the tiger lily stands alone.

Remember to alternate the three green color combinations used for the leaves and veins. Forget reality—you are an artist!

The bee skep center, to form a counterpoint to the brilliant border, must remain soft and undemanding. Use a medium French blue for the sky and a camel brown for the bee skep. Use subtle mottling when dyeing the bee skep wool so that it is not distracting. Although the bee skep is the center of interest, the flower border is the show.

There is no need to dye the black border background. Black commercially dyed wool is readily available and provides a necessary solid background to the variegated flowers and leaves. Prewash this heavily dyed material to be sure it will not bleed in the future. If it bleeds out, simmer it in 2 gallons of water and 1 cup of vinegar to set the dye. Cool, wash, and dry the wool.

Dyeing the Bees

I hope you have the tiny amounts of dark browns for the bees and the beige check needed for the bee wings. I use a black and white check for the upper bee antennae because it runs into the black border. Be sure these tiny areas contrast strongly with all backgrounds or they will be lost.

Dyeing the Bee Skep

You can spot dye the bee skep wool with spent onion shells or Cushing dye. If you opt for onion skins, use the resultant dark rust dye for the divider strips. Oatmeal wool is hard to find; you may substitute camel wool.

Spot Dyeing the Bee Skep with Onion Skins. Spot dye or speckle the camel bee skep wool with onion skins to suggest the texture of woven grasses. Tear an 8-inch piece from the 1/2 yard of camel wool with the selvage to dye deeper rust for the line dividers. Presoak the remaining wool and the 8-inch piece in a wetting agent.

Soak one quart of Golden Globe onion shells overnight in a quart pan of water. Onion shells are not poisonous, so you may use your kitchen utensils. Simmer the shells for $1/2$ hour. You will see the rust color leaching from the skins. Strain off the liquid into a 1-quart pot. Save the shells. If you do not simmer your shells to remove some of the color before spot dyeing your fabric, they will leave dark splotches on your camel wool. You are aiming for a subtle shift of color.

Squeeze out the presoak water from the camel wool, and layer the large piece of wool in a casserole pan. Between the layers, sprinkle spent onion shells and a dusting of salt. Cover the casserole with a lid or aluminum foil, and steam the wool one hour on top of the stove. Check periodically to be sure the pan does not boil dry. Add $1/4$ cup of vinegar-water solution when needed for additional moisture. Permit to cool in the pan so that the color sets.

Rinse off the shells from the camel wool in the sink with the strainer closed! Onion shells are pesky; they cling to the wool and clog up the drain. Keep rinsing in warm water until the wool is free of shells, then (and only then) spin out the rinse water in your washer. You may dry the wool in the dryer until damp and fluffy. Then finish drying it on a rack.

Dye the remaining 8-inch camel piece with the quart of onion skin dye you set aside earlier. Add $1/2$ cup of vinegar and 1 teaspoon of salt. Simmer the wool until you have achieved the darker value for the dividers. When the dye is almost exhausted, throw in some gold scraps for the golden rust daffodil and tiger lily sections. Cool the wool in the pan. Wash, rinse, and dry the wool.

Spot Dyeing the Bee Skep with Cushing Dye. If onion skins are too messy or unavailable, spot dye the camel bee skep with Mummy Brown dye. Use a very light dye solution, $1/64$ teaspoon MummyBrown to 2 cups of boiling water to dissolve the dye. Add 1 teaspoon of salt and $1/4$ cup of vinegar to the dye solution. Use spot dyeing techniques for spotting the bottom as well as the top of the wool (see chapter 6). Add 1 cup of the dye solution to 1 quart of water for dyeing the bottom half of the wool, scrunched down in a 2-gallon dye pot. Use the other cup of the dye solution to pour over the top of the prewetted crowded wool. Process for 30 minutes. Cool, wash, and dry.

The dark dividers may be overdyed with $1/32$ teaspoon Mummy Brown. Presoak 1 ounce of the camel wool, and proceed with open pan dyeing (see chapter 6).

Dyeing the Sky

To complement the warm rich colors of the flowers, I use a soft French blue for the sky. For 6 ounces of white wool ($1/2$ yard), use $4/32$ teaspoon Robin's Egg Blue, $2/32$ teaspoon Copenhagen Blue, and $1/128$ teaspoon Yellow in 1 cup of boiling water. Add 1 teaspoon of salt, and process this wool with the open pan dyeing method, adding $1/4$ cup of vinegar near the simmer stage (see chapter 6) and another $1/4$ cup 15 minutes later. Stir well and process 1 hour.

Dyeing the Trellis

For 8 ounces ($2/3$ yard) of wool, dissolve $2/32$ teaspoon Ecru in 1 cup of boiling water plus 1 teaspoon of salt. Use the open pan dyeing method, adding $1/2$ cup of vinegar at intervals (see chapter 6).

Dyeing the Flowers

If you are dyeing the swatches for "Beehive" flowers and leaves, you will need $11/3$ yard of white wool torn selvage to selvage in four 12-inch strips. Then tear with the selvage sixty 3-by-12-inch strips to dye in graduated colors using the jar dyeing process. The remaining white wool can be used for the white flowers and overdyed for off-whites and beige tones needed for shading.

If you do not care to dye, you may purchase Maryanne Lincoln's "Country Colors" that match my color choices (see Materials section).

Dyeing the Rose and Poppy. Dissolve $2/32$ teaspoon Egyptian Red for a six-value swatch using the jar dyeing method.

Dyeing the Dogwood. There is no need to dye for these flowers because you are pulling colors from other flowers. Use Rose (#2 value, light pink) for the white petal outlines. Use pale yellow-green for the dogwood center shading.

Dyeing the Pansy. Using jar dyeing for a six-value swatch (six 3-by-12-inch strips), dissolve 1/32 teaspoon Purple and 2/32 teaspoon Rose for the dye solution.

Dyeing the Trumpet Flowers. Dissolve 2/32 teaspoon Rose for the dye solution. Dye six values (six 3-by-12-inch strips) using the jar dyeing method.

Dyeing the Zinnia and Daffodil. You will need eight 3-by-12-inch strips for all the yellows needed in "Beehive." Dissolve 2/32 teaspoon Old Gold and 2/32 teaspoon Yellow for the dye solution. When jar dyeing these swatches, also prepare another jar with a 1/32-teaspoon dye solution of Yellow to overdye a neutral or light green tweed of plaid (use various scraps if you have them) for some of the flower centers. Process this jar with the above eight jars.

Dyeing the Calla Lily, Apple Blossoms, and Daisies. There is no need to dye for these flowers. Pull the colors from other parts of the rug. Scraps of off-white, beige, and ecru will shade the white flowers. Deepest gold will be used for the lily "candle" and daisy centers. Use medium gold for the apple blossom centers.

Dyeing the Petunia and Iris. Dissolve 2/32 teaspoon Purple and 3/32 teaspoon Copenhagen Blue for a six-value swatch (3-by-12-inch strips). Use deep gold for the petunia center and medium gold for the iris beards.

Dyeing the Tiger Lily. Overdye #3 value and #4 value gold scraps with onion skin dye when you are dyeing the bee skep dividers, or tint the wool lightly with Rust dye.

Dyeing the Magnolia. Make a dye solution of 2/32 teaspoon Maroon for jar dyeing six values of deep maroon to pale maroon for the magnolia petals. Use a strip of "divider" brown for the branch.

Dyeing the Leaf Greens

You will need three groups of green shades for the leaves: blue-greens, warm greens, and yellow-greens.

For the blue-greens, dye a six-value swatch of six 3-by-12-inch strips. Dissolve 2/32 teaspoon Myrtle Green for the dye solution to jar dye these values.

For the warm greens, jar dye a six-value swatch of six 3-by-12-inch strips using a dye solution of $2/32$ teaspoon Green.

For the yellow-greens, dissolve $2/32$ teaspoon Bronze Green and $1/128$ teaspoon Yellow for a dye solution to jar dye a six-value swatch of six 3-by-12-inch strips.

Hooking "Beehive"

Hooking the Bees

Begin "Beehive" by hooking the bees. Use #6 cut. Alternate rows of brown and dark brown in the tail, ending with a dark brown stinger. Hook the black head, body, antennae, and legs. Use a camel check or plaid for the small veins in the bee wings, then hook the large white wings and the small beige wings. Please note that it is necessary for this tiny amount to be darker than the trellis so that it will show up against this area. Draw the scrap for the small beige wings from the calla lily wool. Use a black and white check for the antennae of the upper bee so that they do not disappear into the black background.

Hooking the Bee Skep

Using #6 cut, outline the "rope" base and hook the horizontal dividers in the bee skep with the darker medium brown wool. The hive itself can be hooked in #6 or #8 cut with onion-speckled camel or oatmeal wool.

Be careful *not* to begin and end your strips at the same place. The dividers have to begin and end at the outside edges. For this reason, avoid as many cuts as you can at the outside edges, and instead bury them in the body of the skep. A row of cuts along any edge looks terrible and weakens the work. Fill in the doorway with black wool.

Hooking the Sky

Outline the sky, beehive, and bees with sky blue wool cut in #6 or #8 strips. Place your initials in a lower corner with one of the medium colors in your border. In undulating rows, hook the sky.

Hooking the Trellis

Using #8 cut, hook the trellis with three rows of off-white strips, beginning with the rectangle around the sky, then hooking three rows around the outside edges. Hook in the block dividers.

Hooking the Flowers and Leaves

I like to hook the border flowers in sequence. The green leaves alternate blue-green, warm green, and yellow-green. The secret to success is balance and variety. Use scraps of brown from the bee skep to add variety to the woody stems. Hook the leaf veins in contrasting greens, either lighter or darker. I used #8 cut, but you can substitute #6 for the small areas or all the flowers and leaves.

Hooking the Rose. Hook a loop or two of black in the center of the rose. Outline the curl of the center petal with the lightest Egyptian Red (1), then decrease in value to light (2) red and medium (3) red. This completes the center petal. Using the deepest red (6), hook a zigzag row (indicating folds inside the lower petal), then reverse your shading from (5) red to (2) red to complete the right side of the rose. To finish the left side of the rose, begin with the deepest red (6) against the black throat, and gradually decrease in value to (4) and (3) reds, completing the left side of the rose.

Hook the tendril and stem in medium brown. Hook dark green veins and blue-green leaves.

Hooking the Dogwood. Hook several loops with deep gold for the centers. Using pale yellow-green, outline the center and make the small extensions. Now outline the dogwood flower in light pink and fill in with white. Hook the stem in medium brown. Use a warm green for the leaves and dark green for the veins.

Hooking the Pansy. Hook two loops of black in the center, and surround them with one row of vivid yellow-green. Hook the black pansy "eyes" in black, then outline those petals in (1) and (2) pale red-purple. The right, left, and center petals increase in value, (3), (4), and (5) into the eyes. Hook the upper rear petal in (5) or (6) red-purple, completing that petal in (3) red-purple. Hook the bud in the lightest (1) red-purple.

Hook the stems and veins in light warm green, and finish the leaves in blue-green wool.

Hooking the Trumpet Flowers. Place vivid yellow-green in the centers of both flowers, and surround these areas with the darkest value (6) of rose. Outline the outer edge of the trumpet furl with the lightest (1) shade of rose. Gradually increase the value of rose, (3), (4), and (5) into the centers. Fill in the forward curl of the petal with (2) rose. Hook the rear lower flower in (6) rose, and the forward lower flower in (5).

Hook the trumpet flower leaf veins in dark yellow-green and the leaves in light yellow-green.

Hooking the Zinnia. Hook the center of the zinnia with a bright yellow-green center (I overdyed a check), surrounded by the deepest gold (6). In a wavy fashion, I alternated rows of yellow from the lightest (1) to dark (5) gold, beginning with several rows of the palest (1) yellow around the center. Gradually increase the values of your petals alternating light and dark until the last row is hooked in (6) deep gold.

Hook the zinnia leaves in blue-green with pale green veins.

Hooking the Calla Lily. Hook the "candle" in deep gold. Outline the lily throat with beige, and fill in the center with off-white. The remaining lily corolla is hooked in white. Hook the base of the flower in beige.

Hook the leaves in yellow-green with darker green veins.

Hooking the Petunia. Hook the center of the petunia in a vivid yellow-green. Radiate out from this center with the darkest purple (6). Outline the petunia with the lightest purple (1). Using (4) purple, hook behind the radiating lines, then hook (3) purple and one row of (2) purple. End with the previously hooked (1) outline.

Use warm green for the leaves and dark green for the petunia leaf veins.

Hooking the Poppy. Begin hooking the poppy with a large black center. Outline the outer edge of the flower with one row of (2) Egyptian Red. Increase in values (3), (4), (5), and (6), ending at the black center. Hook the outer side of the flower, beginning at the (2) edge, and increase in values (3) and (4). Hook the bud with (4) red.

Use yellow-green for the stems and serrated leaves. Use warm green for the veins.

Hooking the Tiger Lily. With #6 cut dark green, hook the stamens. Hook the pistils in deep maroon (6). Each petal is outlined with a gold or rust-gold row, using a deeper rust where petals overlap. Fill in the front petals with the lighter gold or golden rust and the back petals with a slightly darker shade.

Hook the veins in dark green and the leaves in medium warm green.

Hooking the Apple Blossoms. Hook the centers in deep gold, and outline with pale yellow-green in a star-like configuration. Outline the front white flower in off-white to contrast with the adjoining white flower. The bottom flower peeking out is hooked in light beige.

Use various shades of yellow-green and warm green for the leaves and dark greens for the veins.

Hooking the Magnolia. With the darkest shade of maroon (6), hook the center. From this center, hook in medium dark (5) veins. Hook the outlines of all the petals and the turned-up edges with the lightest maroon (1). Fill in rear petals with (2), (3), and (4) light maroon, making each petal a slightly different tone.

Use dark medium brown for the stem and light blue-green for the leaves. The veins are hooked in pale warm green.

Hooking the Daffodil. Use yellow-green for the sta-men (I overdyed a check). Fill in the throat of the trum-pet with dark rust, a lighter golden rust from the tiger lily, (5) gold, and finally ending with (1) light yellow for the outside frilled edge. Outline the trumpet and all the petals with (5) deep gold. Use (1) light yellow for the trumpet. Alternate (2), (3), and (4) yellows for the petals.

Hook the stems and leaves in two shades of yellow-green or warm green.

Hooking the Iris. Begin by hooking one row of (4) gold beards on the three lower petals. Then outline each petal with (1) purple, including the upper ruffles. Each petal calls for dramatic shifts of color to define the petals. In the upright and down-turning forward petal, hook the deepest (6) purple around the beard and inside the upright ruffle. Decrease in values (5), (4), and (3) purple to the (1) outline. Hook a row of (1) pale purple next to the right and left gold beards, then increase the values (3), (4), and (5) toward the center petal. Hook the rear upright petal and the forward curl in (2) and (3) medium values of purple.

Hook the leaves in shades of blue-green.

Hooking the Daisies. Make each center a (5) deep gold. Alternate off-white and white for the petals. The bud is white.

Hook the leaves in yellow-green with deeper green veins.

Hooking the Border

Complete the border blocks by hooking one row of black around each flower motif. Then outline the outside edge of each block (against the trellis). Fill in, following the contour of each flower until the background hooking straightens out at the outline edge.

PATTERN

"Victorian Birdhouse"

2 by 3 feet

MATERIALS

Maryanne Lincoln will provide your wool needs with the colors suggested below, if you do not care to dye for "Victorian Birdhouse" (see Sources).

Birdhouse
1/4-yard piece (28 1/2 by 18 inches) of butter yellow wool, Dorr Sunflower.
Shingled dormers. Scraps of (two 3-by-12-inch pieces) light gray tweed overdyed gold. 12-by-12-inch light gray tweed and 12-by-12-inch piece of white wool to be dyed Terra Cotta *or* one 8-value swatch of Sturbridge Red (R12-6T), Maryanne Lincoln, for the porch and dormer roofs and chimneys.
Entries. Scraps of charcoal black.
Roofs. Scraps of dark gray and gray plaid.
Details. Scraps of deep gold, coral, black, and black and white check.
Trim and post. 1/4 yard white wool.

Birds
Male bird. 1 sheet (12 by 24 inches) deep navy.
Details of the male bird. Two 3-by-12-inch strips of bright blue and two 3-by-12-inch strips of medium dark blue.
Eye. Scraps of black and black and white check.
Female bird's breast. Two 3-by-12-inch pieces of silver gray.
Eye and beak. Black scraps.
Female bird's body and wings. Two 3-by-12-inch pieces of light brown and two 3-by-12-inch pieces of overdyed light brown tweed *or* New Basket Brown, Maryanne Lincoln (values #1, 2, and 3).

Sky
1 yard of pale aqua wool spotted with cream.
Cloud. Scrap of white and off-white.

Background trees
12 ounces (1 yard) of white wool dyed and spot dyed in four shades of green (1/4 yard each).

Twig lattice border
1/3 yard of warm brown wool *or* Seasoned Brown, Maryanne Lincoln (values #2 and #3).

Border leaves
Scraps of three shades of dark green *or* Forest Green, Maryanne Lincoln (values #1 and #2, 3-by-12-inch strip each).

Border berries
Drawn from the male bird blues.

Corner flowers
Scraps of coral, deep gold, and medium rust.

Initials, date, and berry vine
Scraps of overdyed warm brown check.

DYES

(Cushing's Perfection Acid Dye)

Robin's Egg Blue

Old Gold

Spice Brown

Silver Gray

Golden Brown

Medium Brown

Yellow

Reseda Green

Dark Green

Terra Cotta (if desired)

Victorian Birdhouses

Walking home from school every day, I passed a Victorian birdhouse. It was a fascinating miniature of the main house, complete with scrollwork, gables, shingled roof, porches, and balustrades. Alas, it was demolished at the same time as the residence.

The exuberance of American Gothic architecture (or Carpenter Gothic) grew in part from new discoveries in technology. Bending wood under steam and the steam-powered scroll saw gave the builder scope to invent new and elaborate decorative devices, such as scrolls, curlicues, and cutouts. This never-before-possible embellishment was known as "gingerbread."

My Victorian birdhouse is an apartment house for purple martins. We all know that male purple martins are not purple. They are black with royal blue flashings. The female purple martin is very drab beside her flashy mate. I used three colors to depict her feathers: dip-dyed silver gray throat fading to a white breast, brown tweed body, and light brown wings and tail. Don't let reality stop you. If you want to exercise artistic license, by all means, dye the males purple and hook the berries in the border vine in the same shade.

To replicate the golden days of summer, wash some yellow into all the background shades. Having an overall wash of yellow ties the colors in with the center of interest, the Victorian birdhouse.

Tearing the Wool

Because "Victorian Birdhouse" is hooked mostly with #6 cut, tear all the wool with the selvage.

Dyeing for "Victorian Birdhouse"

"Victorian Birdhouse" is based on a yellow and blue color scheme (which combined makes green). All the shades are infused with a golden glow. The sunshine is provided by a wash of gold in the sky and a touch of yellow in some of the green shrubbery. I wanted to invoke the warmth of a summer day.

Dyeing the Rust Chimneys, Porch Roof, and Flowers

To dye an eight-value swatch, dissolve 1/4 teaspoon Terra Cotta in 1 cup of boiling water. Process with eight 3-by-12-inch pieces using the jar dyeing method, only instead of using 1/2 cup dilutions, follow the directions below to obtain deeper shades for the chimneys, trim, roof, and flowers.

Using three 1-quart pans, place 1 teaspoon of salt in each one. In one pan, place 1/2 cup dye solution for two 3-by-12-inch pieces of gray tweed. In the second pan, place 1/4 cup dye solution for two 3-by-12-inch pieces. In the third, place 1/4 cup dye solution for four 3-by-12-inch pieces.

Process for open pan dyeing, adding 2 tablespoons of vinegar at fifteen-minute intervals after the simmer stage. Process 1 hour or longer for deepest values, adding more vinegar if needed.

The deepest two strips will be used to hook the chimneys and outline the dormers. The medium value will be used for the porch roof and to outline the flowers. The paler shades will be used to hook the flowers and trim on the tower.

Dyeing the Birds

Purchase the shades of navy and black needed for the male birds.

For the female breast and feathers, purchase or dye as follows. To dip dye the silver gray, prepare 1/128 teaspoon Silver Gray, 1/2 teaspoon of salt, and 1 tablespoon of vinegar in 2 cups of simmering water in a 1-quart dye pot. Presoak two strips (3 by 12 inches) of white wool. You will need only 1 inch of pale gray before fading to pure white in hooking the breast, so immerse just 4 inches of the strip in the simmering dye bath. Hold it there, slowly lifting and lowering the wool to avoid a strong line of demarcation. You want the gray dye to fade gently into the white area. When the pale shade is achieved, remove the wool from the dye bath, cool, wash, and dry it.

Use two strips (3 by 12 inches) of light brown wool and two strips (3 by 12 inches) of light brown tweed for the female wings. To dye, dissolve 1/32 teaspoon Spice Brown dye in 1 cup of boiling water. Add it to a 1-quart dye pot with a sprinkle of salt and a splash of vinegar. Immerse two presoaked white strips and stir to saturate all surfaces before immersing the two tweed strips. Add heat and simmer thirty minutes or until the light brown shade is obtained. Cool, wash, and dry the wool.

Dyeing the Sky

Presoak 1 yard of white wool. Dissolve in 1 cup of boiling water 3/32 teaspoon of Robin's Egg Blue and 2 teaspoons of salt. You will predye the aqua sky before redyeing with a very pale shade of Old Gold. Add the dye solution to a 2-gallon dye pot filled three-fourths full of warm water. Immerse the white wool, and work the fabric. Heat to simmer, and add 1/2 cup of vinegar. Stirring the wool, simmer fifteen minutes or until the dye is completely taken up. Remove the wool and squeeze it out; do not rinse it. Scrunch the wet wool back into the dye pot. Now add grains of Old Gold (1/128 teaspoon dissolved in 2 cups of boiling water and 1/4 cup more of vinegar) to the wet wool, spot dyeing the top. Steam this wool, adding more water if needed, for a half hour to set the pale gold shading. Cool in the dye bath, wash, and dry.

Dyeing the Background Trees

Tear a 1-yard piece of white wool (12 ounces) into four parts. You will need four shades of warm green for the lower shrubbery and three border backgrounds. The basic dye formula for the 1-yard piece is 2/32 teaspoon Reseda Green, 1 teaspoon of salt, and 1/4 cup of vinegar for open pan dyeing in a 2-gallon dye bath.

Presoak all of the pieces, and dye in the simmering dye bath for thirty to forty minutes or until the dye bath is exhausted. Stir the pieces when immersing to be sure all surfaces are saturated by the dye. You will be spotting and overdyeing three of the pieces later. Remove all of the wool, and spin out in the washer. Do not rinse. Reserve one piece for the lightest shade.

Dissolve $1/32$ teaspoon Yellow in 1 cup of boiling water. Dissolve $1/64$ teaspoon Dark Green in 1 cup of boiling water. In a 1-gallon pan, dissolve $1/64$ teaspoon Reseda Green in 1 cup of boiling water, and add half of the Yellow dye solution in 3 quarts of water. Add 1 teaspoon of salt and $1/4$ cup of vinegar. Immerse one of the previously dyed strips in this dye bath, and simmer for thirty minutes or until the dye bath clears. Remove it. Add half of the Dark Green dye solution to the dye bath, 1 teaspoon of salt, and $1/4$ cup of vinegar. Immerse another dyed strip into this dye bath, and simmer for thirty minutes. Remove it.

Spot dye the last strip with dribbles of the remaining Dark Green dye solution and some of the Yellow dye solution diluted by the addition of 2 cups of boiling water, 1 teaspoon of salt, and $1/4$ cup of vinegar. You do not want this gold dye to be too prominent, but rather a warm spot in the green field. Scrunch down the last strip in a 1-gallon pan, and simmer it for thirty minutes. Cool, wash, and dry all the green strips.

Dyeing the Twig Lattice Border

Presoak $1/3$ yard of white wool. In a 2-gallon dye pot, dissolve $2/32$ teaspoon Medium Brown and $2/32$ teaspoon Golden Brown in 1 cup of boiling water. Add 2 teaspoons of salt. Immerse the wool, lifting and lowering to saturate all surfaces.

I used a brown check for the berry vine, initials, and date. At this time, also dye this small amount (a 3-by-18-inch strip) if desired. Leftover female bird tweed could be substituted.

Work the wool in the dye bath, add $1/2$ cup of vinegar, and simmer for thirty minutes. If the dye bath is not exhausted in thirty minutes, add more vinegar and continue simmering. When the dye bath is clear, cool, wash, and dry the wool.

Hooking "Victorian Birdhouse"

Hooking the Birds

Cut the center of interest—birds, birdhouse, berries, and vine—with #6 cut. The lattice border, sky, and shrubbery is cut with #8, but #6 would do as well.

Begin by hooking the male purple martins. Hook a spot of black and white check for the eyes, then hook in the bright blue accents, top of head, and lines on the wings and body. Outline the wings, beak, and breast with one row of black, and fill in the rest of the body with the dark blue. I added small sections of the medium dark blue in the wings, back, and breast for greater shadowing.

The female beaks and eyes are hooked with black. Hook a line of light brown around the head and a necklace of the darkest gray around the neck. The upper part of the breast is the medium shade of gray fading to white near the tail. Striate the back and upper wing with light brown and tweed, ending with a tweed tail and wing tips.

Hooking the Birdhouse

Outline the house, porch, dormer details, entry holes, support, and post with white wool. Be sure that every line is straight, or the house will list! When hooking the last row of white roof lines, skip out every two loops into a third one-loop row to simulate drop spindles. I used this technique on the outline of the tower roof as well. This jumping out creates a space in which to hook one row of black between the spindles, carrying the wool behind the single loop. Merely skip behind the white loop and fill in the row. This technique avoids all the tiny cuts that would otherwise result.

At this time, fill in behind the porch supports with black and white check to simulate gingerbread fretwork. Hook in the outlined entry holes with charcoal black. Hook the house butter yellow, adding the tower detail with deep gold and coral. Use overdyed gray checks in the dormers (if desired). Hook the rust roofs and the chimneys, adding the gray roof areas last. Using the deep gold, hook one line in the indentations of the support post, then fill in the post with white.

Hooking the Twig Lattice Border
To keep your rug straight and provide a line to bump against when hooking the background, you must first hook in the inner border, then the outer border lines, completing the twig lattice. Now that you have stabilized your edges, return to the background.

Hooking the Sky
I placed a drifting white cloud in the sky to break up the monotony. Hook in this shape with white, underline it with the most golden shade of your aqua sky, and underscore the whole thing with one strip of aqua gold dipped in black coffee. Yes! It was a serendipitous accident that was exactly what was needed.

Outline the sky area, and hook the sky in wavy horizontal rows, burying the ends in various places in the field to avoid having a line of cut edges on either side. (I can't say this often enough!)

Hooking the Background Trees
Save half of the lightest green for the upper border corners. Hook in the upper trees in a wavy fashion with the lightest green mixed with medium light green. Outline the middle shrubbery with a dark line or two, and fill in with mixed medium shades of green. Throw in a light line here and there for highlights. End the row of shrubs at the bottom with the darkest shade of green. Fill in the bottom trellis with the remaining darkest green.

Hooking the Berry Vine
Add the date, initials, and berry vine with the overdyed brown check. Hook in the groups of three berries: light, medium, and dark blue. Using alternate greens, add the veins and dark green leaves. This background will be hooked with the medium greens left over from the trees

and shrubbery. Fill in the lower border corners with the same shade.

Hooking the Upper Border

With a scrap of gold, hook the flower centers. Outline the flower with medium rust, and fill in the flower with coral. Use the same dark greens for the leaves that were used in the berry vine. Complete the upper corners with the remaining light green. Finish the upper border with sky blue behind the lattice.

Hearth and Home

Increased prosperity led to more leisure time, which gave rise to home hobbies. In an age without radio or television, magazines provided entertainment, and women's periodicals printed craft ideas and patterns of all kinds. The abundance of craft supplies was astounding.

At the same time, advertising was born after the Civil War when production caught up with demand and the technology of color printing was introduced. From this flood of colored advertising, a new Victorian hobby was created.

Collecting Victorian vignettes was a popular pastime for young and old. Colorful reproductions were found on advertisements, greeting cards, and printed material of all kinds. Love and friendship, whimsical animals, flowers, and birds were favorite subjects. Known as scrap art, these pictures were cut out and pasted in scrapbooks or used to fashion holiday ornaments. The designs in this chapter were inspired by these sentimental reminders of a gentler past.

PATTERN

"Welcome Friends"

21 by 31 inches

MATERIALS

The wool swatch numbers indicated below are Jane Olson's (McLain) swatches. You may purchase your wool from Jane Olson (see Sources) if you do not care to dye.

Hands
Lady's hand. 12-by-12 inch piece of white wool to be dyed light flesh *or* #63 Jane Olson swatch.
Gentleman's hand. 9-by-12-inch piece of bone wool to be dyed dark flesh *or* #28 Jane Olson swatch.
Cuffs, flowers, and finials. 18-by-14 inch piece of white wool.
Woman's sleeve. 9-by-12 inch piece of silver gray wool.
Man's sleeve. 9-by-12-inch piece of navy blue wool.
Ring, cuff link, and flower centers. Scraps of gold wool.

Flowers
1/3 yard of white wool for 4 shades of burgundy *or* #24 American Beauty Jane Olson swatch. 1/4 yard (18 by 28 1/2 inches) of white wool for 3 shades of rose *or* Light American Beauty, Jane Olson swatch.
Flower centers. Scraps of yellow-green wool.

Lettering
1/4 yard (18 by 28 1/2 inches) of white wool to be dyed medium rose.

Leaves
1/4 yard (18 by 28 1/2 inches) of white wool to be dyed, painted, and spot dyed or 4 pieces (7 by 18 inches) each of pale blue, pale yellow, pale green, and natural to be dyed medium shade of green by Jane Olson.

Veins
Scraps of overdyed maroon plaid.

Trellis
3/4 yard of off-white wool or Dorr 100.

Background
1 1/3 yards of white wool to be dyed dark green.

DYES
(Cushing's Perfection Acid Dye)
Egyptian Red
Mummy Brown
Taupe
Silver Gray
Cherry
Crimson
Maroon
Old Rose
Dark Green
Yellow
Reseda Green

Friendship

Friendships, warm and dear, are as important now as in the day of our sentimental forebears. In a gentler age where symbols spoke as loudly as words, offering one's hand in friendship, asking for a lady's hand in marriage, and a heart held in a hand all indicated abiding love.

The welcome mat was always out and, placed by the front door, greeted guests. My "Welcome Friends" handclasp, under a latticed portico, is surrounded by burgundy roses, complimenting unconscious beauty in the "language of flowers."

Roses meant love, and each variety spoke volumes. Red roses announced true love. White symbolized purity. Yellow suggested a decrease of love or even infidelity, and pink complimented graceful beauty. Expensive and hard to grow, roses were widely popular and became the symbol for an age. As a motif of love, roses were painted, embroidered, tatted, crocheted, and hooked to decorate the home.

© Pat Hornafius 1990

"Heart and Hand"

This popular motif of abiding love was used in many early Victorian craft forms.

Tearing the Wool

You will tear the wool for "Welcome Friends" with the selvage for #6 and finer cuts. The trellis wool and background may be torn with the selvage (for #6 cut) or from selvage to selvage (for #8 cut). Tear the wool as follows:

Lady's hand
> Four 3-by-12-inch strips.

Gentleman's hand
> Three 3-by-12-inch strips of bone wool.

Lady's sleeve
> One 9-by-12-inch piece.

Burgundy flowers
> Four 7-by-12-inch pieces.

Rose flowers
> Four 7-by-18-inch pieces.

Lettering
> One 18-by-28½-inch piece.

Leaves
> Four 7-by-18-inch pieces.

Dyeing for "Welcome Friends"

Dyeing the Hands

For the lady's hand, dissolve $1/128$ teaspoon Egyptian Red and $1/128$ teaspoon Mummy Brown in 1 cup of boiling water. Presoak the four 3-by-12-inch strips. Add $1/2$ teaspoon of salt to each of three 1-quart jars. Two strips will be dyed in the third jar for the lightest value. Add half of the dye solution to jar one for one strip of 3-by-12-inch wool. Dilute the remaining dye solution by adding water to make one cup and add half of this solution to jar two. Add water to make one cup and place the entire solution in jar three. Add presoak water to half fill the jars and stir well. Immerse one strip each in jars one and two, and two strips in jar three. Work the wool well, and process.

Repeat the jar dyeing process as above for the three bone wool strips for the gentleman's hand. Presoak the bone strips. Dissolve $1/128$ teaspoon Egyptian Red and $1/128$ teaspoon Mummy Brown in 1 cup of boiling water. Use half of the dye solution in jar one for one bone strip and the remainder for jar two for two strips of bone wool. Process, using the jar dyeing method, with the lady's hand pieces.

When the hand strips have cooled, overdye the darkest strip of the lady's hand with grains of Taupe dye using the open pan dye process. No need to add more salt or vinegar. This will tint the taupe shade needed for the lines between the fingers and hands and the shadow of the lady's thumb and ring. Cool, wash, rinse, and dry the wool.

The lady's sleeve is a 9-by-12-inch piece of silver gray wool. Dissolve 1/64 teaspoon Silver Gray in 1 cup of boiling water, and proceed with the dip dyeing method. Add 1/2 teaspoon of salt and 1/4 cup of vinegar. Dip dye in three shades.

Dyeing the Burgundy Flowers

Presoak four 7-by-12-inch pieces of white wool for the burgundy flowers. Dye each of the four shades in a separate pan using the open pan dyeing method. Add 1/2 teaspoon of salt to each pan before adding the dye solution.

Pan one, dark maroon
   4/32 teaspoon Maroon.

Pan two, dark burgundy
   1/32 teaspoon Cherry, 1/32 teaspoon Crimson, and 2/32 teaspoon Maroon.

Pan three, medium burgundy
   1/32 teaspoon Cherry, 1/32 teaspoon Maroon.

Pan four, light burgundy
   1/64 teaspoon Cherry, 1/64 teaspoon Maroon.

Maroon reds have a very slow takeup; they will need to be simmered longer and will take more vinegar in the dye process. Use at least 1/2 cup of vinegar for each pan, added gradually in fifteen-minute intervals. Simmer for forty-five minutes, and cool in the dye pan. If the dye has not been exhausted by then, remove the wool and, using clear water, set the dye with 1/2 cup more vinegar. Immerse the wool and bring it to a boil. Simmer fifteen minutes. Again, cool in the dye pan. Wash, rinse, and dry the wool.

Dyeing the Lettering

Presoak the 18-by-28-inch strip. Using the open pan dyeing process, dissolve $3/32$ teaspoon Old Rose and $3/64$ teaspoon Egyptian Red in 1 cup of boiling water. Add 1 teaspoon of salt. Process forty-five minutes to an hour. Use $1/2$ cup of vinegar added gradually at fifteen-minute intervals. Permit to cool in the dye pan.

Dyeing the Rose Flowers

Presoak four 7-by-18-inch pieces of white wool. Dissolve $1/32$ teaspoon Old Rose and $1/64$ teaspoon Egyptian Red in 1 cup of boiling water. Using the open pan or jar dyeing method, add $1/2$ teaspoon of salt to each dye vessel. Use three dilutions for four shades of light pink to barely pinkish white. Cool, wash, rinse, and dry the wool.

Dyeing the Leaves

First dye all the leaves with very light Reseda Green. Tear four 7-by-18-inch strips. One piece will remain very light green. Two will be painted yellow-green through medium green to dark green, and one will be overdyed with spots of yellow and dark green.

Prepare three dye solutions. Dissolve in separate containers $1/32$ teaspoon Reseda Green, $1/32$ teaspoon Yellow, and $1/64$ teaspoon Dark Green in 1 cup of boiling water each.

In a 2-gallon dye pot, place the Reseda Green dye solution with 1 teaspoon of salt. Add all the prewetted white wool pieces, and thoroughly saturate. Work the wool, gradually heating the dye pot. Add $1/4$ cup of vinegar at the simmer stage. Continue to work the wool and add $1/4$ cup more vinegar ten to fifteen minutes later. Process with open pan dyeing, and cool in the dye bath.

Remove the cooled wool and squeeze out the clear dye bath, but do not rinse.

Place two pieces in a casserole pan, and following the directions for "Painting Green Leaves" in chapter 6, use the Yellow and Dark Green dye solutions.

Spot dye the remaining piece with dots of Yellow and Dark Green. Follow "Spot Dyeing" directions in chapter 6.

This will give you a variety of green leaves.

Trellis Material

There is no need to dye this wool. Use off-white wool or Dorr 100.

Dyeing the Background

Presoak 1 1/3 yards of white wool. Dissolve 1/32 teaspoon Yellow and one full package of Dark Green dye in 1 cup of boiling water. Add 1 tablespoon of salt to a 2-gallon (or larger) dye pot. Immerse the wool, lifting and lowering it several times to be sure all the surfaces receive the dye. Bring to a simmer. Then, holding the wool out of the dye bath, add 1/2 cup of vinegar. Swirl it around, and drop the wool back into the dye bath. This is a heavy load of dye and will need another 1/2 cup of vinegar twenty minutes into the dyeing period. Again, lift out the wool before adding the vinegar. This avoids dark splotches on your green wool. Occasionally stir and readjust the wool as it simmers. If the dye bath is not exhausted after forty-five minutes of simmering, add another 1/2 cup of vinegar. Permit the wool to cool in the dye bath. Wash, rinse, and dry.

Hooking "Welcome Friends"

I cut all my off-white trellis material and dark green background material with #8 cut. This works out perfectly for the latticework and frame and speeds up the process. I did, however, cut the dark green interior of the trellis with #6 cut because of the smaller space; #8 cut bulged too much. The flowers and leaves were cut with #6, but I used #3 and #4 cuts for the brilliant centers, pale stems, and white flowers. Use #3 cut for outlining the white eyelet sleeve trim with silver gray and #4 cut for the hands.

Hooking the Hands

Begin the lady's hand by hooking the gold ring, outlined with flesh taupe. Outline the fingers with flesh taupe, and fill in her hand with the pale flesh color, shadowing the fingers in the medium flesh shade. Add fingernails in a light rose shade cut with #3 blade. Outline the gentleman's hand with dark flesh wool and fill in with the lighter flesh color. Hook his nail dull pink. Because the sleeves are buried in flowers, plan to hook them later, but do hook in the eyelet trim, maroon band on the lady's hand, and the cuff on the gentleman's hand.

Hooking the Flowers

The burgundy roses use four shades of burgundy (#6 cut), plus the lettering rose and the deepest shade of pink. Hook from dark to light, being sure to make a lighter shade touch the dark background (so that it won't get lost). Alternate light to dark and dark to light for the pink flowers. Radiate out from the yellow center with #3 cut yellow-green scraps for more interest. The lightest shade of pink used in the flower is almost white. This provides crisp definition. Hook the white flower "bells" (#4 cut), then cap with the palest green (#3 cut). Use this same green and cut #3 for the tiny stems and branches.

Hooking the Leaves

Alternate various shades of green for the leaves to keep them distinct. Use a variety of shades for the veins. When hooking the painted wool, start with a yellow-green end at the tip of the leaf, and hook to the deeper greens touching the flowers. Remember to cut off the brilliant gold ends for the flower centers, or your leaves will look like they are dying!

Hooking the Lettering

Hook one row of Dark Green (#8 cut) at the base of the letters to keep them straight. I cut the lettering wool with #6 cut, making two rows for the small letters and three rows for the capitals and the *l* in "Welcome." While you are hooking the letters, outline with one row of background dark green (#6 cut) to define the letters and keep them true. Now fill in the interior of the letters, and join the letters together by hooking horizontally.

Hooking the Border

Before hooking in more of the background, it is important to stabilize your edges to keep the rug straight.

Hook four rows of dark green down each side and across the bottom (with #8 cut), then fill in to the lettering. Now, starting with the off-white wool, hook four rows up each side and across the top (#8 cut) of the trellis. Carry three of these rows into the trellis frame as you hook the sides, so that the border will be a part of the curve and not be chopped off at the edges.

Having provided the frame, now hook one row (#8 cut) of latticework diagonally across the frame. Hook very close to keep the lines straight. Diagonal hooking is difficult! Then hook the other direction, crossing over the single rows as you go from side to side. The slight crossover will not cause potential pullouts and makes a strong rug. Tiny cuts not only would look choppy, but also could easily pull out. Fill in behind the trellis with dark green #6 cut strips. Do not attempt to use #8, as it is too bulky and would distort the latticework. Outline the lattice squares with #6 dark green strips to maintain the shape, then fill in the center. I alternated the directions of hooking, filling in the squares, to keep the latticework from twisting out of shape.

Completing the Background

Outline the hands, flowers, and leaves with Dark Green (#6 cut). Following the contour of these shapes, continue to fill in several rows.

Now it is time to hook the finials below the trellis. Use #4 cut to maintain the curves. Define the turnings with one small row (#4 cut) of light gray. Outline the finials and the inside of the frame with several rows of dark green. This hooking will be worked into the contouring lines surrounding the center of interest, then joined to flow harmoniously together with the outer border rows.

PATTERN

"Kitten Basket"

2 by 3 feet

MATERIALS

If you do not care to dye, Maryanne Lincoln and Dorr Mill Store will supply you with the needed wool (see Sources).

White kitten
1 ounce of white wool dip dyed silver gray.

Brown kitten
1 ounce of rusty brown wool dyed in 3 shades.

Kitten details
Scraps of pink, white, black, and off-white wool.

Basket
3 ounces of white wool dyed warm brown *or* N4-6T #3, Maryanne Lincoln "Country Colors."
1 ounce of white wool dyed warm golden brown *or* N4-6T #4, Maryanne Lincoln "Country Colors."
2 ounces of brown check *or* 2 ounces white wool overdyed warm brown, *or* N4-6T #1, Maryanne Lincoln "Country Colors."

Roses
2 ounces of graduated strip dyed "ribbon" rose *or* 2 sets of Dorr Mill Store 6-13 Watermelon Potpourri swatches.
10 strips (3 by 12 inches) for graduated strip dyed gold *or* use 2 sets of Dorr Mill Store 6-30 Buttercup Potpourri swatches.

Rose details
Scraps of black, maroon, acid green, and rose spotted yellow wool.

Leaves
2 ounces of graduated strip dyed yellow-green wool *or* 2 sets of 6 swatches (3 by 12 inches) Apple Green, Maryanne Lincoln "Country Colors."

Ribbon border
4 ounces of light pink wool.
4 ounces of medium pink wool.
4 ounces of dark pink wool.
4 ounces of white wool.

Background
16 ounces of white wool dyed medium blue *or* 1½ yards of Dorr Mill #6356 Blue.

DYES
(Cushing's Perfection Acid Dye)

Silver Gray

Strawberry

Egyptian Red

Yellow

Reseda Green

Dark Green

Bronze Green

Golden Brown

Medium Brown

Mummy Brown

Robin's Egg Blue (if needed)

Copenhagen Blue (f needed)

or

(PROChem WashFast Acid Dye)

WF Acid Jet Black #672

WF Acid Yellow #135

WF Acid Sun Yellow #119

WF Acid Fuschia Magenta #349

WF Acid Br. Turquoise #487

WF Acid Brilliant Blue #490

Tearing the Wool

If you are dyeing the entire rug, you will need 2 yards of wool for the center of interest, 1¹/₄ yards for the background, and 1¹/₄ yards for the ribbon border. Tear and cut with the selvage, as cuts finer than #8 are used except where noted.

Dyeing for "Kitten Basket"

In dyeing wool for "Kitten Basket," we pulled out all the stops in dyeing techniques: graduated strip dyeing, dip dyeing, spot dyeing, mottled dyeing, and accordion fold "pin" dyeing. You will redye, overdye, and mottle every fabric for true Victorian extravagance! For the various dye techniques, see chapter 6.

Dyeing the Kittens

The white kitten and the paws and face of the rust kitten take only ¹/₂ ounce, or two 3-by-12-inch lengths. You will dip dye one 3-by-12-inch strip with grains of Silver Gray, a sprinkle of salt, and a splash of vinegar in a 1-quart dye pot half filled with boiling water. Dip dye in thirds from very pale gray to medium light gray. This color defines the chin, ear, and shadows of the white kitten.

The rust kitten will use overdyed warm brown (one 3-by-12-inch strip) from the basket handle and overdyed brown check from the basket outline. Use grains of Mummy Brown to overdye the small strip taken from the basket handle. Dip dye it as above.

Dyeing the Basket

I use accordion fold dyeing for this section to highlight and shadow the basket weave. Use straight pins to secure these folds in 2-inch and 3-inch loops. Presoak 2 ounces of white wool or two 3-by-57-inch lengths. Because I use #8 cut for the basket material (¹/₄-inch strips), I tear the white wool from selvage to selvage. Pin in accordion folds 2-inch loops on one side (which will become 4 inches wide when unpinned) and 3-inch loops on the other side (6 inches when unpinned). Dissolve

1/32 teaspoon Medium Brown and 1/32 teaspoon Golden Brown in 1 cup of boiling water. This is the basic dye solution for the basket color. In a 1-gallon dye pot, place 1 quart of water, half of the dye solution, and 1 teaspoon of salt. Immerse the folded wool and work the dye bath. Bring to a simmer and add 1/4 cup of vinegar. Dye the folded pieces of wool for forty-five minutes or until takeup. Cool and remove, squeezing out the dye bath. Do not remove the pins. Watch your hands!

Now add the remaining dye solution plus 1 teaspoon of salt to the dye pot. The water level should remain very low. Wearing rubber gloves, immerse the 2-inch section in the dye bath, holding it in the dye up to the pins. Be sure the previously dyed 3-inch loops are held above water level. Simmer, and add a splash of vinegar if the dye does not take up quickly. Remove when the dye bath clears. Cool and squeeze out the dye bath. Again, do not remove the pins.

In the meantime, add 1/64 teaspoon Yellow, 1/2 teaspoon of salt, and water to a 3-inch level in a small dye pot. Immerse the previously dyed 3-inch loops into this dye pot, again holding the loops above the pot and immersing only to the pin level. Simmer this color until takeup, adding a splash of vinegar from time to time. After cooling the wool, remove the pins. Voilà! See your cleverly shaded basketweave wool! If you begin hooking correctly with the dark areas, this will hook up into light (pin areas), medium (golden areas), and dark (warm brown areas) to simulate the bulge of the horizontal weave and the dark area behind the vertical slats.

Dyeing the Basket Outlines
For this area, dye a 2-ounce piece of brown and white check or white wool with 1/32 teaspoon Medium Brown and 1/32 teaspoon Golden Brown in a 1-quart dye pot with 1/2 teaspoon of salt and 1/2 cup of vinegar. Simmer for thirty minutes. Cool, wash, and rinse the wool. This darker fabric cut with a #6 blade will define and outline the basket rows, trim, and handle outlines.

Dyeing the Handle and Basket Trim

The twisted basket trim uses half warm brown and half golden brown (1 ounce each). Tear with the selvage for #6 cut. Prepare two warm brown dye baths, one with 1/64 teaspoon Medium Brown and 1/64 teaspoon Golden Brown and the other with 1/64 teaspoon Medium Brown and 1/32 teaspoon Golden Brown. Add 1 teaspoon of salt to each small dye pot. Immerse a 1-ounce piece of wool in each bath. Bring to a simmer (ten minutes), and add 1/2 cup of vinegar to each dye pot. Process the wool. Cool, wash, and rinse. These shades plus a little of the dyed check will also be used in the rust kitten.

Dyeing the Pink Roses and Ribbons

The pink roses can be hooked with Dorr Potpourri swatches 6-13 Watermelon. You will need two sets of six swatches each, light to dark values. Since you will dye the light, medium, and dark pinks for the ribbons, however, I will give you the wool allowance and dye instructions for all the pinks.

The same dye formula will be used for light, medium, and dark pink for the roses and ribbons. The roses will require pinks ranging from very light to very dark, if you are dyeing them. Tear ten 3-by-12-inch strips of wool with the selvage, as you will be using #6 or finer cut. You will use graduated strip dyeing for the five shades of pink needed for the roses.

For the ribbons (three shades), divide 1 yard or 12 ounces of white wool into thirds, and tear with the selvage into three pieces. Presoak the wool. The dye formula will be used in different strengths for each piece. I will give you sufficient dye amounts to dye the strips for the roses as well.

In a 1-pint Pyrex measuring cup, dissolve 1/4 teaspoon Strawberry and 2/32 teaspoon Egyptian Red dye in 2 cups of boiling water. You will add vinegar to the dye bath later. Heat 1 gallon of water. One-eighth of the dye solution will be used to create the light pink ribbon wool (1/3 yard) plus two 3-by-12-inch wool strips for the roses. Add 1 teaspoon of salt and one-eighth of the dye solution (or $1/32$ teaspoon Strawberry and $1/128$ teaspoon Egyptian Red) to the gallon of water. Add the wool. Lift and stir before applying heat. Bring to a simmer (fifteen minutes), and add a total of a $1/4$ cup of vinegar gradually at fifteen-minute intervals. Process the wool for forty-five minutes. Let the wool cool in the dye bath.

For the medium pink wool, use one-fourth of the dye solution (or $2/32$ teaspoon Strawberry and $1/64$ teaspoon Egyptian Red). Proceed as above, adding two 3-by-12-inch strips for the roses along with a $1/3$-yard piece for the ribbon.

For the dark pink, use three-eighths of the original dye solution (or $3/32$ teaspoon Strawberry and $1/32$ teaspoon Egyptian Red). Immerse the last $1/3$-yard ribbon piece and two 3-by-12-inch strips for the roses. Process as above. Spin out the wool, and check the color definition. Reimmerse with additional dye if the values are not distinct. You want gentle contrasts, not strong ones.

You now have one-fourth of the original dye solution remaining. To the rest, add 2 cups of water and 1 teaspoon of salt to dye the two darkest strips. Remove $1/2$ teaspoon of this solution and reserve for dyeing the two lightest strips for the pink roses. Drop two 3-by-12-inch strips into the pot. Lift and stir to be sure that they are totally saturated before applying heat. Bring to a simmer, and add $1/4$ cup of vinegar gradually at intervals. Continue to simmer until the dark shade you desire is achieved (about forty-five minutes). Cool in the dye bath.

The last two strips will be the very lightest pink (really almost white), needed for the edges of the pink roses. Using the reserved dye, process as above.

Cool, wash, and rinse all the processed pieces of wool.

Dyeing the Yellow Roses with PROChem WashFast Acid Dye

You may use two sets of Dorr Mill Store 6-30 Buttercup Potpourri swatches for the yellow roses, or using the graduated strip jar dyeing method to dye ten 3-by-12-inch pieces of white wool torn with the selvage.

Using PROChem WashFast Acid dyes, dissolve $4/32$ teaspoon Yellow #135 in 2 cups of boiling water. In a second cup, dissolve $1/128$ teaspoon Fuschia #349, and in a third cup, dissolve $1/128$ teaspoon Turquoise #487 in 1 cup boiling water each.

Combine the yellow dye with 4 tablespoons of the fuschia dye solution and 4 teaspoons of the blue dye solution. (Note: retain fuschia and blue dye solutions.) Stir well. Add a drop or two of Synthrapol. Dissolve $1/4$ teaspoon ammonium sulfate in warm water and add to the dye solution. Place $1/2$ teaspoon of salt in each jar.

Presoak ten 3-by-12-inch white wool strips. Use the graduated strip jar method of dyeing for five jars, two strips per jar. You may have to add extra vinegar for complete takeup in jars one and two. Process for one hour, working the wool frequently. Cool in the dye bath.

Dyeing the Leaves

Using Cushing Acid Dyes. Using Cushing acid dyes for the leaves, you will dip ten 3-by-12-inch lengths of white wool in a series of pale yellow-green to deeper green shades. Remember that medium green will not show up against the medium blue background, so keep most of each dip dyed strip on the pale side. The darker ends can also be used for the veins.

In separate cups, dissolve $1/32$ teaspoon each of Bronze Green, Reseda Green, Yellow, and Dark Green in 1 cup of boiling water. Add 2 cups of water to a 1-quart dye pot, and 1 teaspoon of salt and 1 tablespoon of vinegar at simmer. Using the dip dyeing technique, you will dye a variety of yellow-greens by combining the various dyes as you dip dye each strip.

To begin the lightest yellow-green, combine drops of Yellow and Reseda Green dye solutions in a 1-quart dye pot. Lower the strip gradually until the entire strip is saturated with color, then proceed with the dip dyeing techniques, adding more dye solution. Vary the strips by using weak combinations of the dyes for slightly different shades and values. Squeeze out some of the strips and reimmerse in other combinations, always keeping in mind that the light end should be a pale yellow-green. Reimmerse one-third of one end of a pale strip into weak dark green for a stronger contrast against other leaves in the pattern. These dark ends will also serve as veins. You may also want to spot dye some of the light leaves with various shades for more variegation. Combine at will. Have fun!

Using PROChem WashFast Acid Dyes. Using PROChem WashFast Acid dyes for the leaves, dissolve 2/32 teaspoon Yellow #119 in 1 cup of boiling water. To this yellow dye solution, add the remaining fuschia and blue dye solutions you made for the yellow roses. For 2 ounces of presoaked wool or ten 3-by-12-inch white wool strips, dissolve 1/4 teaspoon ammonium sulfate in warm water and add to the dye bath, along with a drop or two of Synthrapol.

Using the jar method of graduated strip dyeing, divide the dye solution into five jars. Process for one hour. You may have to add a teaspoon of vinegar to the darkest colors to get complete takeup. Cool in jars, wash, and dry.

Dyeing the Background

If you do not wish to dye the background, you may use Dorr wool #6356 (1¼ yards). This, of course, will not be mottled.

Using Cushing Acid Dyes. To dye medium blue, dissolve 1/4 teaspoon plus 2/32 teaspoon Robin's Egg Blue, 5/32 teaspoon Copenhagen Blue, and 1/32 teaspoon Yellow in 2 cups of boiling water. If you do not have a pot large enough to take 1¼ yards of material, tear the wool in half and dye it in two batches, using half of the above dye solution for each batch. A 2-gallon dye pot will handle this halved amount very nicely. Fill three-fourths full with water, and add half the dye solution and 1 tablespoon of salt.

Immerse the presoaked white wool, then lift and stir to be sure all surfaces are saturated before dropping the wool back into the pot. You want the wool to be slightly mottled, not strongly variegated, so wait fifteen minutes before adding 1/4 cup of vinegar. Lift the wool out of the dye bath, add the vinegar, swirl, and return the wool to the dye bath. Stir several times to be sure that the dye does not accumulate in any one area. Continue simmering for fifteen minutes, working the wool in the dye bath so that there will be no "hot spots." After fifteen minutes, add $1/2$ cup more vinegar, swirl, and return the wool to the dye bath. Work the wool every ten minutes, and keep gradually adding $1/4$ cup of vinegar until the dye bath is exhausted. Process for one hour. Let the wool cool in the dye bath (this will assist takeup), then wash and rinse the wool.

Repeat for the second batch. If the second batch is a slightly different shade, it will only enhance the variety of the background color. You will mix these two batches when hooking.

Dyeing the Background with PROChem WashFast Acid Dyes. Divide the background wool ($11/4$ yard) into two pieces for ease in handling in the dye pot. Presoak the wool in $1/2$ teaspoon Synthrapol.

Dissolve $1/8$ teaspoon Blue #490 with $1/8$ teaspoon Black #672 in 1 cup of boiling water. Follow the open pan dyeing method. Use an acid solution of 1 teaspoon of ammonium sulfate, 1 tablespoon of salt, and $1/8$ teaspoon Synthrapol in 1 cup of lukewarm water. Divide both solutions in half. You will use half in each batch of wool.

To a 2-gallon dye pot filled half full, add half of the dye solution and half of the acid solution. Stir well. Add half of the presoaked wool, lifting and lowering, working the wool well before applying heat. Very gradually heat the wool, working frequently. From the time of simmer, when the dye begins to take, work more often to avoid blotches. Process for one hour, and cool in the dye bath. Repeat for the second batch of wool.

Hooking "Kitten Basket"

Cut the wool in a variety of cuts. I used #3, #4, #6, and #8 for different parts of the rug. You may follow my guidelines or hook even finer for some of the sections.

Hooking the Kittens

Begin with the white kitten. Using #3 cut, hook the black and white eyes. Hook the nose and mouth with #3 cut medium pink. The head, ears, and chest are defined by the light gray you have dip dyed. Use the deepest shade behind the white paws. Finish hooking the white kitten by filling in with white. I used #4 cut.

To make the tiger stripes in the rust kitten, you will need a very small amount of various browns drawn from the rest of the rug. Hook in the face as you did for the white kitten, adding white whiskers with #3 cut. Outline the entire kitten with rust wool (#4 cut), using white for the paws and off-white for the chest. Use tiny scraps of check (basket outline) for the stripes at the top of the head and around the face. Alternate rust and basket brown, filling in the body. I used a gold-brown from the basket for inside the ears. You could very well leave the hooking of the rust kitten until you have finished the basket to gain these tiny scraps.

Hooking the Basket

Having cleverly solved the shading problem of the basketweave by pin dyeing, you are now ready to cut the wool. I used #8 cut (1/4-inch strips) for this area.

Cut the overdyed check for the basket outlines with #6 cut. Hook in all the basket outlines, including the trim and handle.

Beginning at the edge of the basket, hook horizontally across the width, skipping over the vertical splats as you go. This will eliminate the need for tiny cuts in each section. If you have begun hooking at the right spot, the dark shadows will appear under the splats and the light spot will appear in the center of the basketweave bulge. If the shading goes off, don't fret. Mine did too. Complete the basket, filling in the handle and trim with half light and half dark strips. Keep the light strips on top of the twist. I used #6 cut. Finish the rust kitten with the remaining scraps.

Hooking the Roses and Leaves

Plan to alternate the distribution of light, medium, and dark pinks when hooking the pink roses. Do the same with the yellow roses. I used #4 and #6 cuts for these areas.

Use the variety of leaf greens to avoid duplicating adjacent leaves. Hook the darkest greens for veins and some leaf outlines.

Hooking the Ribbons

The ribbon border twists around the white and deep pink stripe. Cut the white line with #6 cut and the deep pink inner stripe with #8 cut. Hook in these lines before beginning the twisted ribbon. With #6 cut, hook the ribbon twist, keeping the light pink on top and the medium pink on the underside.

Now you are ready to hook the bow. Outline the bow with #6 white, placing deep pink inside the bows and alternating the loops with light and medium pinks.

Hooking the Background

Outline the entire center of interest with medium blue. I used #8 cut, but #6 will do as well. Following the contour of the shapes, fill in the background up to the inner border stripe.

Hooking the Outer Border

To stabilize the edge, now hook the second white and pink stripe around the outer edge with #8 cut strips. Fill in the outer border with medium blue, adding your initials with deep pink.

PATTERN

"Tussie Mussie and Candy Stripes"

22 1/2 by 32 1/2 inches

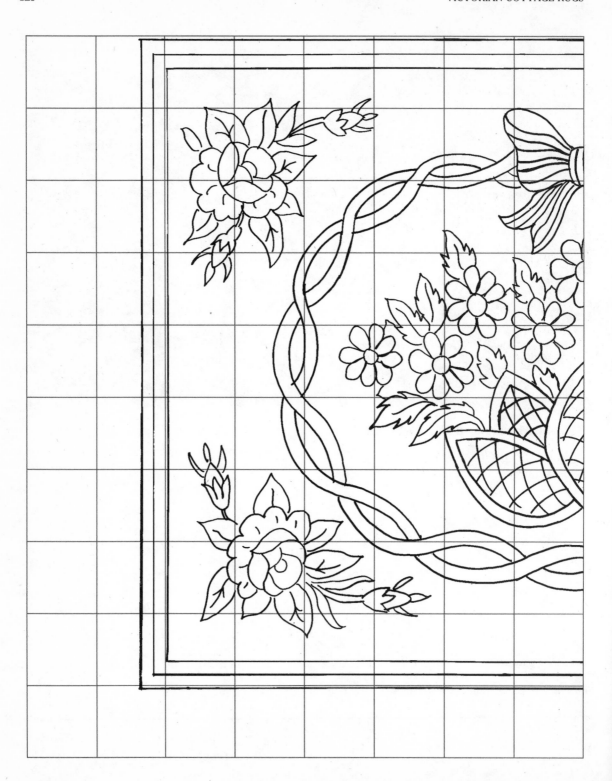

MATERIALS

Wool for this pattern may be obtained from Janet Dobson or any of the master dyers listed in Sources.

Basket
 1½ ounces of medium brown wool *or* 12-by-37-inch piece of white wool.

Inside of the basket
 ¾ ounce of ecru wool *or* 12-by-20-inch piece of white wool.

Flowers
 ½ ounce each of 8 shades of terra cotta, from very light to deep pink wool, *or* two 8-value 3-by-12-inch swatches.

Flower centers
 Scraps of gold, very dark terra cotta, bright green overdyed plaid wool.

Leaves
 Three 6-value 3-by-12-inch swatches of medium to dark blue-green wool, including strips of very light warm green for veins and stamens.

Center background
 6 ounces off-white wool.

Candy stripe ribbon and border
 4 ounces of medium terra cotta wool.
 4 ounces of light terra cotta wool.

Outside border background
 9 ounces of myrtle green wool.

DYES

(Cushing's Perfection Acid Dye)

Golden Brown

Medium Brown

Ecru

Terra Cotta

Buttercup Yellow

Bright Green (if needed)

Dark Green

Green

Myrtle Green

Tussie Mussies

Tussie mussies were small easily transported bouquets, often held in conelike containers, that were tributes to a lady's grace. Through the "language of flowers," tussie mussies could indicate a heartfelt wish or serve as a love letter without words. A single type or a limited variety of flowers conveyed a clear message. In this case, musk roses meant capricious beauty.

Tearing the Wool

I hooked the basket, flowers, leaves, and ribbon with #6 cut. For the background and border stripes, I used #8 cut. Tear with the selvage for #6 cut as follows:

Basket
Tear 1/3 yard of white wool into two pieces: 12-by-37-inch piece for the basket and 12-by-20-inch piece for the inside of the basket.

Flowers
Tear 1/3 yard of white wool into nineteen 3-by-12-inch strips. Save one of the strips for the gold flower center.

Leaves
Tear 1/3 yard of white wool into nineteen 3-by-12-inch strips.

Candy stripe ribbon
Tear 2/3 yard of white wool in half (24 by 28 1/2 inches each) to be dyed light and medium terra cotta.

Dyeing for "Tussie Mussie and Candy Stripes"

Dyeing the Basket

Presoak the 12-by-37-inch basket piece of white wool. Using the open pan dyeing method, dissolve 1/32 teaspoon Golden Brown and 1/32 teaspoon Medium Brown in 1 cup of boiling water. Add the dye solution to a 1-gallon dye pot with 1 teaspoon of salt. Add 1/4 cup of vinegar at the simmer stage and another 1/4 cup of vinegar thirty minutes later. Work the wool, and process 1 hour for complete takeup.

Dyeing the Inside of the Basket

Presoak a 12-by-20-inch piece of white wool. Dissolve 1/32 teaspoon Ecru in 1 cup of boiling water. Process as above.

Dyeing the Flowers

Presoak eighteen 3-by-12-inch strips. Dissolve $4/32$ teaspoon Terra Cotta in 1 cup of boiling water. Use six 1-quart jars for graduated strip dyeing, adding 1 teaspoon of salt to each jar. Place $1/2$ cup of dye solution for the three darkest strips in jar one. Refill the cup with water, and add half of this dye solution to jar two to dye three more strips. Continue adding $1/2$ cup of the diluted solution to each jar, dyeing three strips in each. Process as described in chapter 6.

Dyeing the Flower Centers

Now you will dye the extra 3-by-12-inch strip for the gold centers. Dissolve $1/64$ teaspoon of Buttercup Yellow and $1/2$ teaspoon of salt in 1 cup of boiling water. Use the open pan dyeing method. Gradually add a total of $1/2$ cup of vinegar at fifteen-minute intervals. Simmer for one hour, cool, wash, and dry.

If you have a piece neutral plaid or check, 3 by 12 inches or less, dye this with $1/64$ teaspoon Bright Green as an accent for the flower centers. Also use the darkest terra cotta scraps to add variety to the flower centers.

Dyeing the Leaves

Separately dissolve $3/32$ teaspoon Dark Green, $1/64$ teaspoon Buttercup Yellow, $2/32$ teaspoon Green, and $3/32$ teaspoon Myrtle Green each in 1 cup of boiling water. Presoak eighteen 3-by-12-inch strips. You will dye five shades of medium dark blue-green and one very light warm green strip for stamens and some veins.

Use the open pan method of dyeing. Add 1 teaspoon of salt to each of your four dye solutions. You will gradually add a total of $1/2$ cup of vinegar at intervals to each pan as it is being processed.

In pan one, place $1/3$ cup Dark Green dye solution plus $1/2$ cup Buttercup Yellow solution, and process three strips of wool.

In pan two, place $1/3$ cup Dark Green dye solution with $1/3$ cup Myrtle Green solution, and process six strips of wool.

In pan three, place 1/3 cup Green dye solution with 1/3 cup Myrtle Green solution, and process six strips of wool.

In pan four, place 1/3 cup Green dye solution and 1/3 cup Dark Green solution, and process three strips of wool.

In pan five, place the remaining 1/3 cup Green solution with 1/3 cup Myrtle Green and 1/3 cup Buttercup Yellow, and process three strips of wool. Save 1 tablespoon of this dye solution for dyeing the last strip.

Place the reserved tablespoon of dye solution in pan six, and dye the last strip a pale yellow-green.

Dyeing the Candy Stripes

You will need two pieces (24 by 28 1/2 inches each or half of 2/3 yard) for dyeing two shades of terra cotta. Presoak both pieces.

For the medium terra cotta, dissolve 4/32 teaspoon Terra Cotta dye in 1 cup of boiling water. In a 2-gallon dye pot process with open pan dyeing using 1 tablespoon of salt and 1 cup of vinegar (1/4 cups added at fifteen-minute intervals) for one hour. Cool, wash, and dry the wool.

For the light terra cotta, dissolve 1/64 teaspoon Terra Cotta dye in 1 cup of boiling water. Add 1 teaspoon of salt. Process as above, using 1/2 cup of vinegar.

Dyeing the Outside Border

Presoak 9 ounces of white wool. Dissolve 1/8 teaspoon Myrtle Green dye in one cup of boiling water and add 1 tablespoon of salt. In a two-gallon dye pot using the open pan method of dyeing, process this wool very slowly (it tends to blotch). Thoroughly saturate the wool, and slowly bring it to simmer, working the wool often. Gradually add a total of 1/4 cup of vinegar at fifteen-minute intervals. Simmer for one hour, and cool in the dye pot. Wash, rinse, and dry the wool.

Hooking "Tussie Mussie and Candy Stripes"

Hooking the Basket

Cut all basket wool with #6 cut. Hook the basket outline with two rows and the interwoven centers with one row. I hooked in one direction for the sideways weave, then skipped over these rows when hooking in the other direction. This eliminates tiny cuts that could pull out.

Fill in the spaces with #6 cut ecru wool.

Hooking the Musk Roses

Musk roses mean capricious beauty, so be capricious and hook your roses with a variety of shades. Alternate light, medium, and dark outside rows, saving the darkest for roses touching the off-white background, and using the palest shade of terra cotta for roses nestled in the foliage.

Rose centers are alternately hooked with deep terra cotta and bright green overdyed plaid surrounded by gold. Around these centers, hook radiating shades of light or dark terra cotta. Graduate the colors to the outside row.

I hooked three light roses, three medium roses, and three dark roses, interspersing them throughout the bouquet.

Hooking the Tussie Mussie Leaves

Outline the top of the basket area in medium dark green to define the roses. Alternate the shades of the leaves, using light warm green or dark blue-green for contrasting veins. Include some of the background myrtle green for leaves in the basket.

Hooking the Striped Ribbon

Hook the bow in alternating medium and light terra cotta pink stripes. Use one of the deep terra cotta shades for the outline of the knot and the inside of the bows.

Outline the twisted ribbon frame with medium terra cotta, filling in with one row of light terra cotta.

Hooking the Center

I used #8 cut for the center to match the outside backgrounds, but you could use #6 cut if you prefer. Outline the tussie mussie and ribbon twist with several rows, then fill in with contour hooking. Hook in the spaces between the ribbon twist with off-white wool.

Hooking the Border Roses

For greater contrast with the myrtle green background, plan to graduate your colors from dark centers and folds to the lightest pinks on the outside edges. I hooked the buds in the dark terra cotta shades.

Hooking the Border Leaves

Use your darkest three shades of blue-green wool for the border leaves to be sure of a contrast against the myrtle green background. Pale warm green strips are used for some veins, small leaves, and stamens.

Hooking the Striped Outside Rows

To keep your rug straight, now is the time to hook the three outside rows, alternating light pink, medium pink, and light pink. This will stabilize the rectangle before adding the border background.

Hooking the Border Background

Outline the corner flowers, leaves, ribbon twist, and outside border rows with myrtle green. Hook in your initials at this time. Then continue outlining until the rows touch the corner flowers. Now contour your hooking horizontal to the outside perimeter until the background border is completed.

Adding the Fringe

I used a yarn fringe on the ends of this rug. If you wish to add this Victorian touch, see chapter 11 for instructions.

PATTERN ───

"Sea Fans and Shells"

2 by 3 feet

MATERIALS

Wool for this pattern may be obtained from Janet Dobson or any of the master dyers listed in Sources.

Urn

Outlines and dividers. 1 ounce of dark gold wool.
Inside dividers. 1 ounce of medium gold wool.
Centers. 1 ounce of light gold wool.
Urn handles and base shadows. 3-by-12-inch strip of very dark gold wool.

Whelks

Scraps of tan wool.
Scraps of rusty brown, white, off-white, and tan check wool (from sea snails).

Sea grapes

Two 3-by-12-inch strips of two shades of very dark maroon wool.
Stems. Scraps of background green wool.

Sea fans

Lower One. 3-by-12-inch strip each of 2 shades of medium light maroon wool.
Middle Two. 3-by-12-inch strips each of 3 shades of old rose, mauve, and light maroon wool; one 3-by-12-inch strip of pale gold wool, spot dyed with very light Egyptian Red.
Upper Three. 3-by-12-inch strips each of the four shades listed above for middle sea fans in even paler values.

Scallop shells

Scraps of white, off-white, 4 shades of gold, rusty brown, and tan check wool drawn from other parts of the rug.

Background

9 ounces of seafoam green wool *or* 3/4 yard of white wool to dye Myrtle Green..

Sea snails in border

2 ounces of rusty brown wool.
2 ounces of tan check wool.
2 ounces of white wool.

Background border

8 ounces of light sand beige wool *or* 2/3 yard of off-white wool to dye ecru.

DYES

(Cushing's Perfection Acid Dye)

Yellow

Old Gold

Mummy Brown

Myrtle Green

Maroon

Old Rose

Egyptian Red

Ecru

Lavender

Blue

Victorian Sea Motifs

In the Victorian fever of botanical discovery, ladies turned their investigation to the sea. Proper attire for "sea rambles" was described in magazines and books on the subject. Collecting sea mosses, ferns, and seaweed, the intrepid naturalists donned woolen stockings, sturdy boots, gloves, and hats and, tucking up their skirts, waded into tidal pools and clambered over rocks. One wonders how many fell in.

Bringing home their treasures, the beachcombers dyed the sea foliage, pressed it between blotters, and dried it. They combined these dried arrangements with shells, purchased from dealers or collected, to create sea "trophies" with which to grace the parlor.

Sea compositions were also a subject for scrapbooks, whose covers were decorated with shells. Artful arrangements, poetic sayings, and botanical information all combined to give Victorians an educational entertainment to pursue in their evenings by the fire. A young Queen Victoria often presented her sea scrapbooks as gifts to friends.

Ornamental shellwork reached its height at mid-

"Cornfield at Night with Shells" is my adaptation of an antique rug from New England, circa 1860.

century. Whalers and sailors in the China trade brought back exotic shells from the Pacific Rim, as well as "sailors' valentines" (shell mosaics enclosed in mahogany boxes) from the West Indies. The rage for shellwork led to such novelties as shell-covered vases, hairbrushes, pincushions, and clocks. Nothing was safe from encrustation.

Not to be outdone, rug makers also took up the rage by depicting exotic shells in their own hand-drawn designs. If the mantlepiece could display souvenir shells, why not the hearth rug?

Tearing the Wool

I cut all but the background and border wool in #6 or finer cuts. You will need 2/3 yard of white wool for the urn and sea snails, and 1/3 yard of off-white wool for the sea grapes and sea fans. Tear the wool with the selvage as follows:

Sea snails
Two 12-by-28 1/2-inch pieces (tear 1/3 yard of white wool in half).

Urn
Nineteen 3-by-12-inch strips of white wool.

Sea grapes
One 3-by-12-inch strip each of off-white and tan check wool.

Sea fans
Eighteen 3-by-12-inch strips of off-white wool.

Dyeing for "Sea Fans and Shells"

You must enjoy dyeing for this one! Varying values and shades of rose, cream, maroon, and mauve require a dribble of this and a drop of that to achieve a variety of similar, but different, pale colors. Use open pan dyeing or jar dyeing, whichever you prefer.

Dyeing the Urn

Presoak nineteen strips of 3-by-12-inch white wool. Dissolve 2/32 teaspoon Old Gold, 2/32 teaspoon Yellow, and 1/64 teaspoon Golden Brown dyes in 1 cup of boiling water. You will divide this dye solution as follows:

Darkest gold
1/4 cup dye solution for one strip.

Dark gold
1/4 cup dye solution for three strips.

Medium gold
1/4 cup dye solution for six strips.

Light gold
1/8 cup dye solution for four strips.

Pale gold
1/8 cup dye solution for five strips.

The pale gold strips are needed for sea fans and scallop shells. Reserve them.

Using the jar or open pan method of dyeing, add 1 teaspoon of salt to each dye vessel. After the dye bath comes to a simmer, gradually add 1/4 cup of vinegar at fifteen-minute intervals. Use 1/2 cup for medium shades. The dark shades will require about 1 cup total of vinegar to exhaust the dye bath. Process for one hour, and cool the wool in the dye bath.

Dyeing the Sea Grapes

Dissolve 2/32 teaspoon Maroon dye in 1 cup of boiling water. Presoak one 3-by-12-inch strip of off-white wool and one 3-by-12-inch strip of tan check (from the sea snail wool). To a 1-quart dye pot, add the dye solution and 1 teaspoon of salt. Fill the vessel half full of water, and immerse the strips. Work the wool to fully saturate the fibers. This is a heavy load of dye that will take 1 cup of vinegar, added gradually at fifteen-minute intervals after the simmer stage to takeup. The dye may not be exhausted after one hour, but turn off the heat and cool in the dye bath. To fully set the color, simmer the dyed strips in 1/4 cup of vinegar and 1/2 quart of fresh water for fifteen minutes. Cool, wash, and dry the wool.

Dyeing the Sea Fans

Presoak eighteen 3-by-12-inch strips of off-white wool.

You will need a variety of colors for the sea fans. Make a 1-cup dye solution of each of the following dyes to mix and match for a number of shades and values. Separately dissolve 2/32 teaspoon of Maroon, 1/32 teaspoon of Egyptian Red, 1/32 teaspoon of Old Rose, 1/128 teaspoon of Lavender, and 1/128 teaspoon of Blue each in 1 cup of boiling water.

For the lower fans, use 1/2 cup of the Maroon dye solution to dye two strips.

For the middle fans, use: 1/4 cup Old Rose plus 1/4 cup Egyptian Red for two strips; 1/4 cup Maroon plus 1/4 cup Lavender for two strips; 1/2 cup Lavender plus 1/2 cup Blue and 1/4 cup Old Rose for two strips; and 1/8 cup Egyptian Red diluted in 1/2 cup water to spot dye one pale gold strip.

For the upper fans, use 1/8 cup Old Rose plus 1/8 cup Egyptian Red for three strips; 1/8 cup Maroon for three strips; 1/8 cup Lavender plus 1/8 cup Old Rose for three strips; 1/8 cup Old Rose for two strips; and 1/8 cup Egyptian Red diluted in 1/2 cup water to spot dye three strips of pale gold.

Fill each dye vessel three-fourths full of water, and add 1 teaspoon of salt. Gradually add a total of 1/4 cup of vinegar at fifteen-minute intervals after the simmer stage until the dye bath is exhausted. Process for forty-five minutes to one hour, and permit to cool in the dye bath.

Dyeing the Background

Presoak 9 ounces (3/4 yard) of white wool. Dissolve 6/32 teaspoon Myrtle Green dye in 1 cup of boiling water. Add 1 tablespoon of salt. Work this wool very thoroughly in a 2-gallon dye bath to fully saturate the wool with dye solution. This color tends to splotch, so apply heat slowly, working the wool. Measure out 1 cup of vinegar. Add 1/4 cup of vinegar at simmer, and gradually add in 1/4 cup more vinegar at each fifteen-minute interval throughout the dye process. Process for one hour, and permit to cool in the dye bath. Wash, rinse, and dry the wool.

Dyeing the Sea Snails

Sea snails need 1/3 yard of white wool, half dyed rusty brown. To dye one 2-ounce piece (12 by 28 1/2 inches), dissolve 1/32 teaspoon Medium Brown, 2/32 teaspoon

Mummy Brown, and $^1/_{32}$ teaspoon Yellow in 1 cup of boiling water with 1 tablespoon of salt. Process for one hour in a 1-gallon dye bath, gradually adding a total of $^1/_2$ cup of vinegar at fifteen-minute intervals, using the open pan method of dyeing.

Dyeing the Outer Border

To dye light sand beige, dissolve $^3/_{32}$ teaspoon Ecru. Presoak $^2/_3$ yard off-white wool. Process with open pan dyeing, using 1 tablespoon of salt. Gradually add a total of $^1/_2$ cup of vinegar at fifteen-minute intervals. Stir often, and cool in the dye bath.

Hooking for "Sea Fans and Shells"

Hooking the Urn

Using #6 cut, hook the outline and shell dividers with dark gold. Use very dark gold for the handles and base shadows. On either side of the dividers, hook a row of medium gold, then fill in the center with light gold. This will create the appearance of a convex surface.

Finish the urn pedestal alternating dark and light gold, separating each section with a tiny thread (#3 cut) of rusty brown.

Hooking the Whelks

Outline the shell spirals with rusty brown, then fill them in, alternating white, off-white, light tan, and tan check wools from the sea snails. Top the shells with light tan.

Hooking the Sea Grapes

Use #6 cut background myrtle green wool for the undulating sea grape stems. Hook tiny circles (#4 cut) of grapes, alternating your darkest maroon wools. Add several lighter maroon grapes from lower fan wool to highlight the clusters.

Hooking the Sea Fans

Below the sea grapes, shadow in the small areas on either side of the stems with medium light maroon—

lighter than the grapes, darker than the middle sea fans. This will create depth and a strong contrast to the stems and whelks. Alternate the two shades for the lower fans.

For the middle fans around the sea grapes, alternately hook 4 shades of midtones: old rose, mauve, and light maroon, saving the spot dyed cream wool for the center section. This will bring that area forward. Add some rows of light sea fan wool to the middle tones to break up that solid area. The more variety, the better.

Now, above these midtones, hook the lightest values for the upper fans, alternating their position to contrast with the middle fans.

In all levels of sea fans, follow the contour of the edges to create a leafy curlicue line. Before leaving the sea fans, outline the entire urn and composition with one row of #6 cut background green. If you choose to hook the background in #8 cut as I did, this will preserve all the sea fan contouring you worked so hard to create.

Hooking the Scallop Shells

I had a wonderful time creating the scallops! First, hook the upper scallop rim in one row of #6 cut white, then another of off-white (#6). Use #6 cut medium gold for the vertical ridges, hooking from the base directly to the white rim.

Then hook horizontally, skipping under the vertical gold lines. Starting at the top, under the white rim, hook three rows as listed: one row of pale gold, one light gold, and one white. You will have only two loops between the divider lines, so skipping under rather than clipping makes sense.

Because the fan is narrowing, cut the rest of the rows in #4 cut, and continue filling in horizontally, row by row, to the gold base. Hook two rows of pale gold, one row of dark gold, one row of rusty brown, one row of white, and one row of tan check. Complete the scallop rows with white. Hook the hinge with #6 cut tan. Now, outline the scallop with one row of #6 cut background green.

Hooking the Waves

To stabilize the waves before hooking the background, hook two rows of #6 cut background green around the border curves, making a sharp point at the crest of the wave. At the same time, outline the wave in sand beige (#6 cut) in the border. These three rows will keep the shape of the wave crisp and defined.

Hooking the Background

Draw undulating waves across the field of your background. Using #6 or #8 cut, hook in the background, incorporating the central motifs into the "sea."

Hooking the Sea Snails

Before beginning the sea snails, hook two rows of sand beige (#8 cut) at the outside border. This will stabilize your rectangle and provide a base for your snails.

Begin the sea snails with #6 cut white wool strips, leaving an equal size space of 1/4 inch between the spirals. This space will be filled in with one row of #4 cut rusty brown and one row of #4 cut tan check wool. Outline the snails with rusty brown as you begin your spiral into the center.

Hooking the Border

Using #6 or #8 cut, outline the sea snails with sand beige, and continue to fill in between the outer rows and the waves.

Faithful Companions

Framing Your Pet

The border of a pet rug is perhaps as important as the subject itself. Victorian hooked rugs are noted for their elaborate treatment of the framework. All the decorative devices found in other facets of artwork of the time—scrolls, brackets, swags, trellises, and vines—are used to enclose the major motifs. Parquet floor patterns were borrowed for Greek key, interlocking chains, and other complex geometric combinations. Borders often overpowered the center of interest, a far cry from the simplicity of early primitive hooked rugs, which had little or negligible border designs. Gone are the quilt derivations and simple geometrics.

The patterns of Edward Sands Frost interchanged components of the same inner frames and border designs in many combinations. You too can mix and match the elements of the border to suit the dimensions of your pet design. A head portrait can use an inner frame. Full-length views need only an outside border design.

"Jack Russell Terrier," "Golden Retriever," "Yellow Labrador," "Black Labrador," "Corgi," and "White Persian" are six pet portraits that you can duplicate or change to depict your own faithful companion.

PATTERN ———————————————————————————————

"Jack Russell Terrier"

26 by 32 inches

MATERIALS

Dog

Body. 4 ounces of white wool.

Black spots, eye, ear, nose, and tail. 1½ ounces of black wool.

Mouth and inner ear. Scraps of charcoal wool.

Eye patch. Scrap of medium brown wool (same as the line in the border).

Shadows. ½ ounce of beige wool (same as the lines in the border).

Background

16 ounces of dark green wool (also used for two rows of the outside border).

Border

Triangles. 3 ounces of red wool.

Two rows. 3 ounces of beige, bone, or off-white wool.

One row. 1½ ounces of medium brown wool.

Outer triangles. 3 ounces each of checked wool and plaid wool.

DYES
(Cushing's Perfection Acid Dye)

Dark Green

Egyptian Red (if needed)

Dyeing for "Jack Russell Terrier"

Very little dyeing needs to be done for this rug. Most of the fabrics used are found material: white and black for the dog, charcoal for the mouth and ear, red for the triangles in the border, off-white for the outlines, medium brown for the eye patch and one row in the border, and checked and plaid wool for the border.

You may dye the dark green background. If you desire, Egyptian Red can be dyed for the inner border triangles.

Dyeing with Egyptian Red

For 3 ounces of presoaked wool (1/4 yard), dissolve 4/32 teaspoon Egyptian Red in 1 cup of boiling water. Use 1 teaspoon of salt and a total of 1 cup of vinegar gradually added at fifteen-minute intervals. Process for one hour using the open pan dyeing method.

Dyeing with Dark Green

For 1 1/2 yard of presoaked white wool, dissolve 1 package of Dark Green dye in 1 cup of boiling water with 1 tablespoon of salt. Gradually add a total of 2 cups of vinegar at fifteen-minute intervals 1/2 cup at a time. Process for one hour using the open pan dyeing method.

Hooking "Jack Russell Terrier"

Before hooking, see "Cutting the Wool" in chapter 2. "Jack Russell Terrier" uses #8 cut only.

Hooking the Dog

Begin hooking the features of the dog first: the black eye, nose, and ear. Use charcoal wool for the mouth and inner ear. One row of beige defines the jawline. Moving to the body, hook in the black spot and tail band. If you wish to individualize your dog, change the markings, but be sure that not too much black touches the background. Black against dark green is hard to see. Add the medium brown eye patch, if desired. A black eye patch will require a brown eye (think about it).

The beige leg shadows should be hooked next: the back front leg and upper rear leg. Now outline the white body, and fill in following the direction of the contours.

Hooking the Background

It is necessary to stabilize the background rectangle by hooking several rows of dark green around the outside edges before filling in the field. Hook the background in undulating horizontal rows. Place your initials and the date (if desired) in the bottom corners.

Hooking the Border

Stabilize the border by hooking two rows of dark green background wool around the outside edges of the rug. Hook the off-white zigzag lines and one row of medium brown before hooking in the inner red triangles. Outline the triangles first, then hook from side to side, beginning at the base and ending at the point. Next, hook the outer triangles, alternating dark green plaid with beige check. Use the same hooking technique that you used for the red triangles.

"Home Sweet Home"

"Beehive"

"Victorian Birdhouse"

"Welcome Friends"

"Kitten Basket"

"Tussie Mussie and Candy Stripes"

"Sea Fans and Shells"

"Jack Russell Terrier"

"Golden Retriever"

"Yellow Labrador"

"Black Labrador"

"Corgi"

"White Persian"

"Rousseau's Tiger"

"Mallard Decoys"

"Horse Portrait—Diamond Lil"

PATTERN

© Pat Hornafius 1991

"Golden Retriever"

25 1/2 by 39 inches

MATERIALS

Wool for "Golden Retriever" can be purchased from Jane Olson (see Sources).

Dog

Eye. 1 strand of black wool.

Nose. 1 strand of black and white check wool (to contrast with the dark background).

Mouth. 1 strand of charcoal black wool.

Collar. 3-by-12-inch strip of red wool.

Dog's head and body. 3/4 yard of golden brown mottled dyed wool in 4 shades as follows: light shade for the cheek, tail, and front leg outline (1 ounce); medium shade for the body (6 ounces); medium-dark shade for the outlines of the ear and front right leg (1 ounce); dark shade for the rear leg, thigh line, ear folds, and under the chin (1 ounce).

Background

1 1/2 yards of plaid or checked wool overdyed with Dark Green.

Flowers

Centers. Scraps of yellow wool.

Outlines. 10-by-27-inch piece of white wool.

Insides. 10-by-27-inch piece of light pink wool (mottled).

Leaves

Four 6-by-27-inch pieces each, dyed in 4 shades of Reseda Green over white wool.

Veins and stems

12-by-27-inch piece of medium-dark green plaid or mottled wool.

Trellis and outside border

4 ounces of light bone wool.

3 ounces of medium camel or tan wool.

DYES

(Cushing's Perfection Acid Dye)

Medium Brown

Yellow

Mummy Brown

Dark Green

Green

Reseda Green

Egyptian Red

A black Labrador portrait, "Hattie," uses a Frost trellis pattern from "Golden Retriever." Adapt a pattern to depict your pet.

Tearing the Wool

I hooked the entire rug with #8 cut. Tear the wool from selvage to selvage. If you are using #6 cut, tear the wool with the selvage.

Tear 3/4 yard (9 ounces) into four pieces: a 6 ounce piece and three 1-ounce pieces for #8 cut.

If you are using #6 cut (or finer), cut the wool with the selvage in 27-inch lengths:

Light golden brown
6-by-27-inch piece.

Medium golden brown
39-by-27-inch piece.

Medium-dark golden brown
6-by-27-inch piece.

Dark golden brown
6-by-27-inch piece.

Tear 3/4 yard (9 ounces) with the selvage for flowers, leaves, stems, and veins as listed in Materials.

Dyeing for "Golden Retriever"

Dyeing the Dog

Presoak all the dog pieces in a wetting agent. Dissolve
2/32 teaspoonYellow, 2/32 teaspoon Mummy Brown, and
2/32 teaspoon Medium Brown in 2 cups of boiling water
in a Pyrex 1-pint measuring cup. In a 2-gallon dye pot,
add half of the dye solution, 1 teaspoon of salt, and the
39-by-27-inch piece (6 ounces) for the dog body. Lift and
lower the piece to fully saturate the wool. Process with
open pan dyeing, adding 1/2 cup of vinegar, divided in
thirds, at fifteen-minute intervals. Process for forty-five
minutes, and cool in the pan.

For the medium-dark and dark 6-by-27-inch pieces (1
ounce each), divide the reserved 1 cup of dye solution in
two pans as follows: 5 liquid ounces of dye solution and
1/2 teaspoon of salt for the #4 value, and 3 liquid ounces
of dye solution and 1/2 teaspoon of salt for the #3 value.
Process with the open pan method of dyeing. Add 1/4 cup
of vinegar to each pan at the simmer stage.

For the remaining 6-by-27-inch piece, the lightest
value, dissolve 1/128 teaspoon each of Yellow, Mummy
Brown, and Medium Brown, plus 1/2 teaspoon of salt,
and process as above.

Dyeing the Background

For the background, I used a Black Watch tartan plaid
wool, which did not need dyeing, but a green or navy
plaid can be overdyed for this area. Use one package of
Dark Green dye to 2 yards (24 ounces) of presoaked plaid
wool. This is a lot of wool to dye at one time if you do not
have a gigantic cafeteria pot such as mine. If your
largest dye pot is 2 gallons, tear the wool in half and dye
it in two batches. If you plan to do this, dissolve one
package of Dark Green dye in 1 cup of boiling water and
use half for each batch. Add 1 tablespoon of salt to each
batch. After simmering the wool for fifteen minutes,
add 1/2 cup of vinegar to each dye bath. After thirty more
minutes of simmering, lift up the wool to add another
1/2 cup of vinegar, then swirl the dye bath to mix it before

dropping the wool back into the pot. Process for one hour. Cool, wash, and rinse the wool. If the batches do not match exactly, good! Mix the two together when cutting and hooking the background.

Dyeing the Pink Flowers

Dissolve $1/128$ teaspoon Egyptian Red in 1 cup of boiling water. Add $1/2$ teaspoon of salt. Presoak a 10-by-27-inch piece of white wool, and proceed to dye with the open pan dyeing technique, adding $1/4$ cup of vinegar at the simmer stage. Cool in the dye bath, wash, rinse, and dry the wool.

Dyeing the Stems and Veins

Dissolve $2/32$ teaspoon of Reseda Green and $2/32$ teaspoon Green dye in 1 cup of boiling water. In a 1-gallon dye pot, add $1/2$ teaspoon of salt. Immerse the presoaked 12-by-27-inch piece of white wool for the stems and veins. Bring to a simmer for fifteen minutes, then add $1/2$ cup of vinegar, divided into thirds, every fifteen minutes. Continue to process using the open pan method. Cool the wool in the dye pot. Wash, rinse, and dry the wool.

Dyeing the Leaves

Presoak four 6-by-27-inch pieces of white wool. Dissolve $2/32$ teaspoon Reseda Green and $1/32$ teaspoon Green in 1 cup of boiling water, $1/64$ teaspoon Yellow in 1 cup of boiling water, and $1/64$ teaspoon Dark Green in 1 cup of boiling water. In four separate pans, you will use different combinations of these dye solutions. Add 1 teaspoon of salt to each pan.

Pan one
One-fourth of the Reseda Green dye solution.

Pan two
One-fourth of the Reseda Green and half of the Yellow dye solution.

Pan three
One-fourth of the Reseda Green and half of the Dark Green dye solution.

Pan four
One-fourth of the Reseda Green and the remainder of the Yellow and Dark Green dye solutions.

Process the wool pieces, using the open pan dyeing method. Add 2 tablespoons of vinegar to each pan at simmer. Stir often. Permit the wool to cool in the dye baths.

Hooking "Golden Retriever"

Hooking the Dog

Cut all the wool for "Golden Retriever" with #8 cut ($\frac{1}{4}$-inch strips). You may use #6 cut if you prefer, but you may have to use more than one row for the outlines so that they will show up.

Begin hooking with the face details: nose, mouth, eye, ear outline, and ear folds. Hook the red collar before beginning to hook the head. Hook under the chin, and carry this color under the mouth and around the nose. Hook the lighter cheek. Beginning at the chin line, outline the head with the body color. Then, following the contour, fill in the rest of the head.

Using the medium-dark brown wool, hook the front right leg. Hook in the rear leg and thigh line with the dark shade.

Add the light golden brown next in the tail and lower front legs. This will help to distinguish the separate sections and keep them from running together. If you prefer, use this lighter shade for the belly area as well.

Now outline the remainder of the dog with the body color, zigzagging in and out on the chest, forelegs, and belly to simulate fur. Following the contour of the body, continue to hook in the space horizontally, curving your rows around the haunch.

Hooking the Flowers, Veins, Stems, and Leaves

Cut the flower fabric with #6 cut for greater definition. Start with the yellow center, then hook the white outline, and fill in with pale pink.

Hook the veins and stems next, using #8 cut so that they will show up against the background.

Cut the leaves with #6 or #8. Alternating the four shades of green, hook in the leaves. Leaves that fall behind the trellis may have to be hooked later.

Hooking the Trellis

Outline the three rows of camel around the outside edges first in order to stabilize the border rectangle and keep your rug straight. I used #8 cut. Now hook the four rows of light bone wool inside the camel border. Hook the trellis corners with bone and camel wool.

Hooking the Background

Using #8 cut, outline the dog, being sure to get in all the nooks and crannies of the dog fur. Outline the leaves and trellis. I hope the stems show up! Hook in your initials. Now fill in the background, waving your horizontal rows from side to side. This directional hooking will add interest to the dark plaid background. Fill in the trellis corners to complete the rug.

Pattern

"Yellow Labrador"

2 by 3 feet

MATERIALS

If you do not care to dye, you may purchase your wool from Maryanne Lincoln (see Sources).

Dog
> **Body.** 6 ounces of pale tan wool.
> **Body lines.** 1 ounce of dark tan wool.
> **Ear, belly, and tail.** 1 ounce of medium tan wool.
> **Eye and nose.** Scraps of black wool.

Background
> 24 ounces (2 yards) of overdyed navy plaid wool.

Border
> 1 ounce of deep gold wool.
> 2 ounces of light gold wool.
> **Flowers.** 1 ounce of light blue wool.
> **Leaves.** 18-by-24-inch sheet of white wool for 6 values of yellow-green *or* 2 six-value swatches of (3 by 12 inches) Moss Green, Maryanne Lincoln "Country Colors."

DYES
(Cushing's Perfection Acid Dye)

Old Gold

Yellow

Golden Brown

Bronze Green

Copenhagen Blue, Navy, or Dark Green (if needed)

Dyeing for "Yellow Labrador"

Dyeing the Dog

Presoak 1/2 yard of white wool for the dog body and two 1-ounce pieces for the shadows. Dissolve 1/64 teaspoon of Old Gold plus 1/128 teaspoon of Golden Brown in 2 cups of boiling water. Reserve 1 cup of this dye solution for the 1-ounce pieces.

In a 2-gallon dye pot filled halfway, place 1 cup of the dye solution and 1 teaspoon of salt. Stir this dye bath well before immersing the 1/2-yard piece. Thoroughly saturate the wool before applying heat. At the simmer stage, add 1/4 cup of vinegar and work the wool. Proceed with the open pan dyeing method for forty-five minutes. Cool in the dye bath, wash, and dry the wool.

You will dye the two 1-ounce pieces in two 1-quart dye pots. Add 1 teaspoon of salt to each dye pot. Place 2/3 cup of the dye solution in one pan and 1/3 cup in the other. Process these two pieces of wool as above. You should achieve three distinct shades. Cool in the dye bath, wash, and dry the wool.

Dyeing the Border Bands and Scroll Corners

Presoak the two strips for the gold border bands and corners. Dissolve 1/32 teaspoon Old Gold and 1/32 teaspoon Yellow in 1 cup of boiling water. Reserve 1 tablespoon of this solution for dyeing the leaves. Add 1 teaspoon of salt to a 1-gallon dye bath. Immerse the 1-ounce strip for deep gold. Process with open pan dyeing, adding 1/4 cup of vinegar, a tablespoon at a time, at fifteen-minute intervals. Process for 1 hour. Cool in the dye pot, wash, and dry the wool.

Dissolve 1/32 teaspoon Old Gold and 1/32 teaspoon Yellow in 1 cup of boiling water for the 2-ounce strip of light gold. Add 1 teaspoon of salt to a 1-gallon dye bath. Process with open pan dyeing for one hour, adding 1/4 cup of vinegar, a tablespoon at a time, every fifteen minutes. Cool in the dye bath, wash, and dry the wool.

Dyeing the Background

I used a navy plaid wool that only needed to be overdyed with Copenhagen Blue to dye the white areas. You can use any dark plaid available and overdye it to the shade you want for the background. When hooked, undyed plaids are too choppy in appearance to be successful. Overdyeing will cause the colors to blend more harmoniously, and the plaid will have an interestingly textured surface. I have also used a dark green and white plaid overdyed with Navy for a blue-green background.

This is a lot of wool to dye at one time without a very large dye pot. If you are using a 2-gallon pot, tear the wool in half and dye it in two batches. Use the same amount of wool and dye in each batch, and they should match. If they don't, mixing them together when hooking will produce an even more interesting background.

For my navy plaid, I used one package of Copenhagen Blue dye. (Divide in half for two batches.) It is essential that you test the dye color with your plaid. Tear off or cut a small square from the background piece. Dissolve 1/64 teaspoon of the chosen color in 1 cup of boiling water and add to 1 quart of water. Immerse the pre-soaked sample piece. Add a sprinkle of salt and a splash of vinegar, and simmer until the dye absorbs. Rinse the piece and squeeze it out in a paper towel to check the color. Dry, if you have time, to see the slightly lighter shade emerge. If you dislike the resulting color, you have saved 2 yards of precious plaid wool.

Now is the time to fiddle with the overdye and achieve the shade you desire. If it is too bright, add a speck of Black. If it is too light, add a little Navy. When in doubt, overdye the whole piece with Dark Green (one package). You can't go wrong with this color.

Dyeing the Leaves

Tear a 24-by-18-inch piece of white wool into six 4-by-18-inch strips. You will process this wool with jar dyeing. Dissolve 3/32 teaspoon Bronze Green in 1 cup of boiling water. In each of six 1-quart jars, place 1 teaspoon of salt. In jar one, place 1/2 cup of the dye solution and refill the rest of the cup with water. Place half of the dye solution in jar two. Continue diluting by refilling the cup with water and adding half of the dye solution to each successive jar. Process one strip in each jar.

Hooking "Yellow Labrador"

Cut all the wool for "Yellow Labrador" with #8 cut. If you want finer detail in the flowers and leaves, use #6 cut in these areas.

Hooking the Dog

Begin by hooking the nose and eye with black. Use a dark tan to outline the ear, left front leg where it touches the right one, leg shadows, and body lines. Next, hook in the ear, belly, back legs, and one row under the tail with medium tan. Outline the dog with pale tan. Then, following the contour of the body, fill in the dog, forming the rear thigh by curving around this area for several rows.

Hooking the Border Bands and Corners

Hook in the border bands, using one row of deep gold and one of light gold. Fill in the corner scroll shadows in deep gold and complete with pale gold. The flower centers are deep gold, and the petals are mottled light blue. Alternate shades of green for the leaves, using the lightest shade for stems and bud stamens.

Hooking the Background

Place your initials in a corner with one of the shades of green. Begin hooking the background by outlining around the dog, inside the border bands, and around the flowers. To keep the rug straight, hook five outside rows right up to the corner scrolls. Then, using wavy lines, fill in the rest of the background.

Pattern

"Black Labrador"

2 by 3 feet

MATERIALS

Dog
Body. 6 ounces of black wool.
Body lines. 1 ounce of medium dark charcoal gray flannel wool.
Ear, belly, and tail. 1 ounce of dark gray flannel wool.
Nose. Scrap of black and white check wool.
Eye. Scrap of dark brown wool.

Background
24 ounces (2 yards) of terra cotta wool.

Border
1 ounce of deep gold wool.
2 ounces of light gold wool.
Flowers. 1 ounce of very pale pink or white wool.
Leaves, stems, and veins. Eight 3-by-12-inch strips of medium to dark green wool.

DYES
(Cushing's Perfection Acid Dye)

Terra Cotta

Old Gold

Yellow

Reseda Green

Dark Green

The directions given here will produce a terra cotta background. To achieve the medium burgundy background pictured in the color photograph of "Black Labrador," use 3 teaspoons of "Aqualone Wine" Cushing acid dye for 2 yards of white wool.

Dyeing for "Black Labrador"

You will use commercially dyed black wool for the dog body. Find light and dark gray flannel for the outlines and shadows. Scraps from an old gray flannel skirt or slacks are perfect for these small areas.

Dyeing the Background

Dissolve 3$\frac{1}{2}$ teaspoons of Terra Cotta in 1 cup of boiling water for 2 yards of white wool. If you have a huge pot, you can dye the whole piece at one time, but I find it easier to manage 1 yard at a time in a 2-gallon dye pot. Tear the 2-yard piece in half, and dye each separately. Carefully measure half of the dye solution into each of the dye vessels. Add 1 tablespoon of salt to each dye bath. Immerse the presoaked white wool, and lift it several times to be sure that all surfaces receive the dye. Drop the piece into the dye bath and bring to a simmer before adding the first $\frac{1}{4}$ cup of vinegar. Work the wool well. Continue to add $\frac{1}{4}$ cup of vinegar at fifteen-minute intervals, for a total of 1 cup, and process for one hour with open pan dyeing. Cool, wash, and dry the wool.

Dyeing the Border Bands and Scroll Corners

Presoak the two strips needed for the border bands and corners. Dissolve $\frac{1}{32}$ teaspoon Old Gold and $\frac{1}{32}$ teaspoon Yellow in 1 cup of boiling water. Reserve 1 tablespoon of this dye solution for dyeing the leaves. Add 1 teaspoon of salt to a 1-gallon dye bath. Immerse the 1-ounce strip for deep gold. Process with open pan dyeing, for one hour, adding $\frac{1}{4}$ cup of vinegar every fifteen minutes. Cool in the dye pot, wash, and dry the wool.

Dissolve $\frac{1}{32}$ teaspoon Old Gold and $\frac{1}{32}$ teaspoon Yellow in 1 cup of boiling water for the 2 ounces of light gold. Add 1 teaspoon of salt to the 1-gallon dye bath. Process with open pan dyeing for one hour, adding $\frac{1}{4}$ cup of vinegar every fifteen minutes. Cool in the dye bath, wash, and dry the wool.

Dyeing the Leaves

Presoak eight 3-by-12-inch strips of white wool. In two separate measuring cups, dissolve $1/32$ teaspoon Reseda Green and $1/32$ teaspoon Dark Green in 1 cup of boiling water each. Add 1 teaspoon of salt to each measuring cup. You will process the leaves with open pan dyeing, using four 1-quart dye pots and a total of $1/2$ cup of vinegar gradually added at fifteen-minute intervals to each.

Pan one
$1/2$ cup dye solution of Reseda Green for two strips.

Pan two
$1/4$ cup dye solution of Reseda Green for two strips.

Pan three
$1/4$ cup dye solution of Reseda Green and $1/2$ cup Dark Green dye solution for two strips.

Pan four
$1/2$ cup Dark Green dye solution plus the reserved 1 tablespoon of gold dye solution for two strips.

Hooking "Black Labrador"

Cut all the wool for "Black Labrador" with #8 cut. If you prefer, you may cut the flowers and leaves with #6 cut for finer detail.

Hooking the Dog

Begin by hooking in the brown eye and the nose. Use a black and white check for the nose to make it distinct from the black dog. Hook carefully to get the very small white area beside the black face. If placed properly, the small white area creates the illusion of a shiny nose.

Because the dog is black, use the lightest value of gray flannel for the folds. Outline the ear, front leg, and lines in the body.

Using the medium dark charcoal gray flannel, fill in the front right leg, ear, leg shadow, belly, and one row under the tail.

With the black wool, outline the dog's body, then following the contour of the shape, fill in, forming a rear thigh by curving around this area for several rows.

Hooking the Border Bands and Corner Scrolls

Hook one row of the border bands and the corner scroll shadows with deep gold. Hook one row of border bands and the remaining scrolls with light gold.

Hooking the Flowers and Leaves

Using the palest pink or white, outline the flowers and buds. Use a deep gold for the flower centers. Fill in the flowers with the remaining pale pink.

Choose the darkest green for the small stems and veins. Then, alternating the shades of green, complete the leaves.

Hooking the Background

Hook your initials in a corner with one of the leaf greens. Outline the dog with one row of the background terra cotta. To keep your rug straight, hook five rows from the border bands to the outside edges. Outline the flowers, and fill in to the corner scrolls. Add one row inside the border bands to keep them straight, then begin to hook the background with wavy lines, hooking from side to side in a gentle undulating fashion to add interest.

PATTERN

"Corgi"
34 by 24 inches

MATERIALS

Dog

Chest, legs, and belly. 1 ounce of white wool.

Chest, legs, and belly outlines. 1/2 ounce of off-white wool, Dorr 100.

Head and upper back. 1 ounce of dark onion skin rust wool.

Center body and head. 1 1/2 ounces of medium onion skin rust wool.

Lower body. 1/2 ounce light onion skin rust wool.

Inner ear, thigh line, and tail. Very light rust scraps.

Nose and eye. Black scraps.

Eye, ear outlines, and ruff. Dark brown scraps.

Background

10 ounces of medium blue wool, Dorr 6356.

Outside Border

6 ounces of dark medium blue wool, Dorr 6372.

Trellis

4 ounces of off-white wool, Dorr 100.

3 ounces of medium brown wool, Dorr 5.

DYES

Natural onion skins

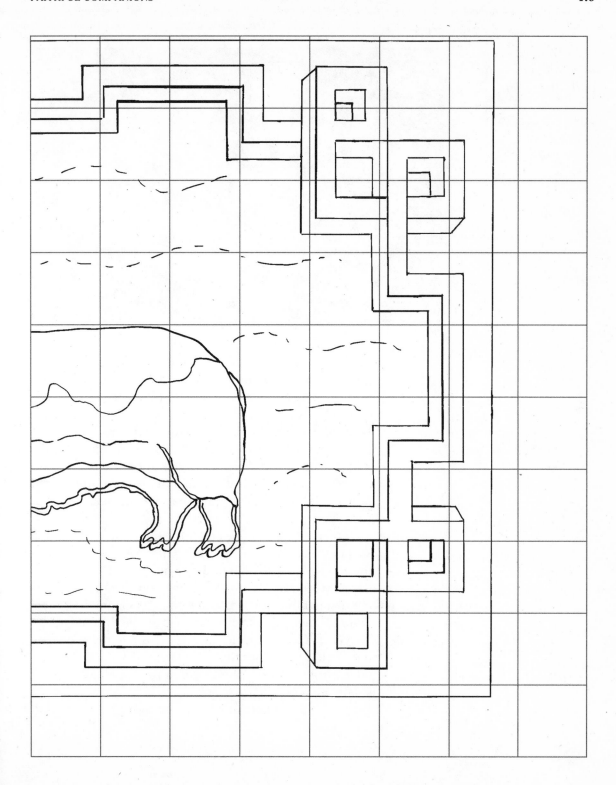

"Corgi Puppy" is an adaptation of a Frost pattern.

I have chosen to make a Pembroke Welsh Corgi, a favorite of the British royal family. You can turn this into a Cardigan Corgi with very few changes.

Dyeing for "Corgi" Using Onion Skins

I dyed the four shades of Corgi rust with onion skins, which produce my favorite shade of rust, but if you do not want the mess, you can use the rust formula given for "Rousseau's Tiger" or another dye formula to match your dog.

Presoak the 1-ounce strip, 1½-ounce strip, ½-ounce strip, and scraps of white wool. Fill a 2-gallon dye pot to the top with dried Golden Globe onion shells, and add 1 gallon of water. My local market saves these skins for me throughout the year when they clean and bag their onions. Placed in a brown paper bag, they can be saved for years. Generally, the drier they are and the deeper their color, the richer the color they produce. However, I once obtained fresh shells which produced a beautiful shade of gold—what a shock!

Soak these skins in water overnight. The next day,

simmer them for one hour, add 1 tablespoon of salt, and immerse the 1-ounce strip. This will produce the darkest shade obtainable when dyeing in the shells. After thirty minutes, add $1/4$ cup of vinegar to the dye pot. Stir it around and check the color. It should be a deep shade of rust. If not, continue to simmer longer. Remove the strip when the dark color appears.

Now add the $11/2$-ounce strip. Again, stir it around and permit the wool to simmer for thirty minutes. Check the color for a medium rust. Dyeing in the shells creates mottling. When you have obtained the medium shade, remove the strip, strain the shells into a colander, and save the "broth."

Return this lighter "broth" dye bath to the dye pot, and add the $1/2$-ounce wool piece. Add another $1/4$ cup of vinegar, and simmer until a light shade of rust appears. Then throw in the scraps of white wool for the very lightest shade. Cool, wash, and dry the wool.

It is only fair to warn you that removing onion skins is very messy! You must pick off the shells before placing your wool in the washer, and they cling stubbornly. I carelessly washed unpicked wool in my washer and had to call the repairman. While I am issuing warnings, never put the shells down the garbage disposal. That, too, required a repair call. What an expensive dye session!

Done with care and patience, onion skin dyeing is easy and fun, but do pick off the skins and rinse the wool thoroughly before placing it in the washer. When the wool cools, run it under warm water in the sink, rinsing off the shells, vinegar, and salt. This not only saves the plumbing, but eliminates the wash cycle. Full of confidence, you may just spin out the excess water before drying the wool. Hanging it outside or on a rack until almost dry will also rid the wool of stubbornly clinging shells. Shake the wool vigorously before finishing the drying in the dryer to fluff the wool.

Hooking "Corgi"
I hooked the entire rug with #8 cut.

Hooking the Dog

With the black strip, hook the mouth and nose. Outline the eye and ears with dark brown. Fill in the black eye, adding a tiny loop of the palest rust for the highlight (#3 cut). Now outline the nose, chest, legs, and belly with one row of off-white wool.

Begin the face by hooking the "mask" with the darkest rust. Place a line of light rust down the nose. Outline the eye sockets with dark rust and hook the jawline before filling in the face with medium rust wool. The ears are hooked with four shades of rust. Use the very lightest scraps for the inner ear, the rear thigh line, and the tail.

Hook the dark ruff at the neck with one or two rows of dark brown, interspersing dark rust, then trail the dark rust across the upper back. Hook the center of the dog with medium rust, and finish with light rust to the belly. Complete the Corgi by hooking the white chest, feet, and belly.

Hooking the Border

Before you begin the background, you must stabilize your edges to keep the rug straight. Hook in the medium brown trellis outline with two rows. Then complete the trellis, hooking three rows of off-white. Add your initials with medium brown wool.

Hooking the Background

Now outline the dog and trellis with the medium blue background color. Hook in wavy, undulating rows across the field, turning your rows and hiding the cut ends throughout the work.

The outside border is completed by hooking four rows around the entire rug with darker blue, then filling in the holes in the trellis.

PATTERN

"White Persian"

35 1/2 by 23 inches

MATERIALS

Cat
Body. 3 ounces of white wool.
1 ounce of white wool dyed 3 shades of Silver Gray.
Eyes. Scraps of black and medium green wool.
Nose and ears. Scraps of light pink wool.

Flowers
2 ounces of light terra cotta pink wool.
1/2 ounce of medium terra cotta pink wool.
Flower centers. 1/2 ounce of maroon wool.

Leaves
3 shades of medium green wool taken from the border wool.
Veins. Scraps of dark green and medium green plaid.

Frame
2 ounces of light gold wool.
2 ounces of dark gold wool (also used for flower centers).

Background
Inner. 9 ounces of deep terra cotta wool.
Outer. 8 ounces of dark tartan plaid.

Border leaves and rows
5 ounces of medium green.

DYES
(Cushing's Perfection Acid Dye)

Silver Gray

Terra Cotta

Reseda Green

Old Gold

Yellow

Maroon

Black (if needed)

"Paisley Cat," a black cat portrait, is surrounded by brilliant paisley motifs, a favorite Victorian design pattern drawn from textiles of the period.

Dyeing for "White Persian"

"White Persian" was a commissioned portrait of a Persian Chinchilla. You could use this pattern to portray any cat breed by changing the shape, colors, and markings. Tipping the fur very slightly by dip dyeing with Silver Gray breaks up the expanse of white, creating tiny spots of gray at the tips of the fur. This must be done very judiciously or the cat will look polka-dotted. Use the medium light gray strip for whiskers and facial markings and the darker gray for body definition and the mouth.

Dyeing the White Cat

The facial fur is cut with #4 and #6 cuts, so rip the wool with the selvage. The white cat was hooked with #6 cut. Tear the 4 ounces of white wool ($1/3$ yard or 12 inches) into sixteen 12-by-$3^1/2$-inch strips. Eight will be left undyed.

Presoak eight of the 12-by-$3^1/2$-inch strips of wool. Dissolve $1/64$ teaspoon Silver Gray in 1 cup of boiling water. Using the graduated pan dyeing method, add $1/2$ teaspoon of salt to three pans. For pan one, use half of the dye solution. Refill the cup with water again and add half the diluted dye solution to pan two. Again refill the cup, and add it all to pan three. Add $1/4$ cup of vinegar to each pan at the simmer stage. Dye the darkest strip and the medium strip using the pan method of processing.

Use the solution in pan three to dip dye the tips of the fur. Holding six of the 12-inch strips, lift and lower only 1 inch of the ends into the weak dye bath. Add $1/4$ cup of vinegar at the simmer stage, and continue dipping until the dye bath is exhausted. These pale tips are all you need for the chinchilla markings.

Dyeing the Terra Cotta

The background behind the cat is deep terra cotta. You will use 9 ounces of wool for the background, and scraps of this wool for the rose shading. You need a total of 1 yard of white wool. I cut the background wool with #8 cut. At this time, also prepare the strips for the roses. I used #8 cut, but you may prefer hooking the roses with #6 cut for greater detail.

From the 1-yard piece, tear off a "quarter yarder" piece ($28^{1}/2$-by-18-inches). You will dye a six-value swatch of Terra Cotta for the flowers. Tear the "quarter-yarder" into seven strips (4-by-18 inches). Presoak all the pieces.

Dissolve $1/32$ teaspoon Terra Cotta in 1 cup of boiling water. Using the jar dyeing method, place 1 teaspoon of salt in each of six jars. Add $1/2$ cup of dye solution to jar one. Refill the cup to the top with water, and add half of this diluted solution to jar two. Fill the cup up again with water, and add half of this solution to jar three. Repeat this procedure for the next two jars, and add all the remaining solution to jar six. Dissolve $1/32$ teaspoon Maroon plus 1 teaspoon salt in 1 cup of boiling water for the remaining 4-by-18-inch piece. Process this jar along with the terra cotta shades. Add 1 tablespoon of vinegar to each jar at the simmer stage.

Presoak the remaining 9-ounce piece of white wool for the inner background. Dissolve $1/2$ teaspoon Terra Cotta dye in 1 cup of boiling water. In a 2-gallon dye pot, add 1 tablespoon of salt and fill three-fourths full (use your presoaking water). Add the dye solution and stir well before immersing the 9-ounce piece. Lift and lower to be sure the wool is thoroughly saturated with the dye. When the wool comes to a simmer, add 1/2 cup of vinegar. Lift the wool out of the dye pot to avoid direct contact with the vinegar, then, swirling the dye bath, lower the wool into the dye pot again. Work the wool thoroughly, and continue to simmer thirty more minutes before adding another 1/2 cup of vinegar. Be sure to lift the wool and swirl the dye bath to avoid unwanted splotches from instant takeup. Simmer for one hour, cool in the dye bath, wash, and dry.

The frame and border (plus leaves) require 9 ounces of wool (3/4 yard). This 27-inch-long piece can be divided in half, to a width of 28 inches. Tear the piece in half again for two 27-by-14-inch pieces for the two shades of gold for the frame.

Dyeing the Frame

Dissolve 3/32 teaspoon Old Gold and 3/32 teaspoon Yellow in 1 cup of boiling water. Use 2/3 cup of this dye solution for the 27-by-14-inch piece needed for dark gold. Use the remaining 1/3 cup of dye solution for the other piece for light gold. Using the open pan dyeing method, add 1 teaspoon of salt to each pan. Immerse the wool, thoroughly saturating it with dye, and bring to a simmer. Add 1/2 cup of vinegar, work the wool, and continue to simmer for thirty minutes. Add another 1/2 cup of vinegar, and continue to process the wool for one hour. Cool in the dye bath, wash, and dry the wool.

Dyeing the Border

Tear the remaining 27-by-28-inch piece of wool in half for two 27-by-14-inch pieces. You will dye one of these pieces Reseda Green for the border. Tear the other piece into three 27-by-4½-inch strips for three shades of green for the leaves.

Dissolve 2/32 teaspoon Reseda Green in 1 cup of boiling water. Presoak one 27-by-14-inch piece of wool for the border. Add 1 teaspoon of salt and the dye solution to a 1-gallon dye pot filled three-fourths full. Immerse the wool and thoroughly saturate it. Process with 1/4 cup of vinegar adding two tablespoons of vinegar every fifteen minutes after the simmer stage. Simmer and work the dye bath for forty-five minutes. Cool, wash, and dry the wool.

Dyeing the Leaves

For the three 27-by-4$1/2$-inch strips needed for the leaves, dissolve $3/32$ teaspoon Reseda Green in 1 cup of boiling water. Using the graduated strip open pan dyeing method, add 1 teaspoon of salt to each vessel. Add $1/2$ cup of dye to the first dye pot. Refill the cup with water, and add half of the solution to the second pan. Add the remaining dye solution to the third dye pot. Immerse the presoaked wool and thoroughly saturate with dye. Process the wool for forty-five minutes, adding two tablespoons of vinegar every ten minutes to each pan after the simmer stage. Cool in the dye pans, wash, and dry.

Dyeing the Outer Background

Plaids are composed of many color combinations. By hand cutting the wool, you can choose the band of color you desire before cutting the wool into #8 cut strips. I found a dark green and red plaid that had yellow lines running through it. By tearing along this yellow thread, I was able to eliminate the bright intrusion when I cut my strips into $1/4$-inch strands. If you have a limited amount of plaid or one that has too much light or bright color in it, you will have to overdye. I have overdyed very bright red and green plaids with black in the past for dark but vibrant variations of black. This is known as "antique" black. The original colors glow through the black overdye, giving life to this otherwise dead color. Plaids can also be overdyed with any other very dark color to enhance what would be an uninteresting background if a solid color were used.

Presoak the wool you are overdyeing in a wetting agent. For 8 ounces or $2/3$ yard of wool, use $3/4$ teaspoon of black dye. Dissolve this dye in 1 cup of boiling water. Pour the dye into a 2-quart dye pot three-fourths full of cool water, and add $1/2$ cup of vinegar. Stir well. You can add more black dye later if needed, but don't go overboard with the first dye solution or your wool may end up solid black.

Immerse the wool, lifting and lowering it to absorb the black dye. Stir thoroughly, then bring the wool to a simmer slowly, stirring frequently. Simmer for forty minutes. Cool in the dye bath for complete takeup. If the wool has not darkened sufficiently, add a little more black dye solution (dissolved in 1 cup of boiling water) to the same dye bath and redye, repeating the original dyeing instructions.

If you have a piece of Black Watch wool or other dark tartan plaid that does not need to be overdyed, you do not have to go through all this.

Hooking "White Persian"

Hooking the Cat

Begin with the face, using #3 cut, and hook a black outline of the eyes. White Persians wear eyeliner. Add the black pupils and a tiny loop of #3 white for highlights. Fill in the eyes with medium green. Hook the nose and inner ear with #4 cut lightest pink and the mouth with #4 cut darkest gray. I used the medium gray #4 cut for the facial fur markings and #3 cut for the whisker dots.

Now begin with the outside edges of the facial fur, using the tip dyed white wool. Hook into the center of the face. Continue this directional hooking, filling in and reversing with the white wool to avoid cut ends in the same place. Outline the ears, down the brow, and the nose with solid white. The tiny line (#3 cut) of light gray under the curve of the mouth indicates the chin.

Before hooking the rest of the cat, outline the outside edges, including the tail, with one row of light gray. Where the tail meets the body, hook another row of the darkest gray to show a definite demarcation.

Hook the chest and back fur in the direction it would naturally fall, again using the gray-tipped white wool. Scatter the tips throughout the back fur.

Hooking the Flowers

The pink roses are hooked in graduated shades of the background color. Use the light pink for the outside petals of the large rose so that it is defined against the white cat. Hook the rose center, using a scrap of maroon (or black), and gradually lighten the rows to the outside edges for the greatest contrast against the background. Hook the buds with light and medium pink.

Outline the large flower with the lightest pink, make the center the deepest gold, and hook radiating lines from the center with medium terra cotta.

Hooking the Leaves
Begin the leaves with dark veins (I overdyed green plaid with Dark Green). Use the deepest shade of medium green for the veins of the lightest leaves. Hook the stems with vein material. Have fun with the leaves—alternate shades, outline with different shades, use your eye to determine placement of color.

Hooking the Frame
Hook two rows of light gold in the inner oval and two rows of dark gold along the outside. The scroll ends are first shaded with the dark gold, then hooked in the light gold. Finish the "crown" on each end with the deepest gold, accented with light gold lines.

Hooking the Background and Border
Before beginning the background of the cat, hook the outer border to stabilize the edges. This will keep the rectangle straight; you won't have to contend with the bulge created when hooking the inner background. Hook three rows of medium green. Now hook in the terra cotta center, outlining the cat, flowers, leaves, and frame before filling in the background, following the contour of the frame.

In each corner are leaves hooked in three shades of medium green. Hook the outside rows and veins with the lightest green. Place your initials in the field with one of the greens.

Outline all the edges with dark tartan plaid before filling in the field, hooking horizontally.

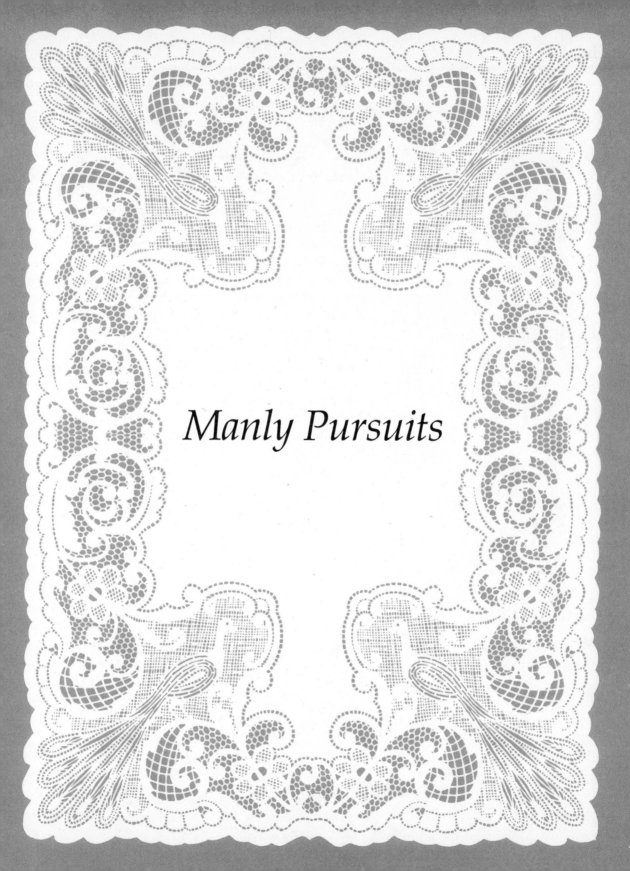

Manly Pursuits

In an era of "sweetness and light," the pervasive reliance on home as the source of all comfort struck some editors as feminizing. To counteract the influence of home and child rearing, they urged Victorian men to take up "manly pursuits."

Exploration and safaris, hunting and fishing, and horsemanship in all its forms were masculine pastimes guaranteed to leave the little woman at home.

Art and literature lured gentlemen to answer the call of the wild. The art of Henri Rousseau portrayed the romance of the jungle with its fabulous fauna and fantastic flora. Racks of horns, stuffed heads, and animal skin rugs were thought to display bravery and manliness in the face of the dangerous unknown. Trophy safaris contributed to the demise of the world's greatest beasts. Today, we revere the endangered species, placing hooked replicas of them on our floors.

"Rousseau's Tiger," "Mallard Ducks," and "Horse Portrait—Diamond Lil" are hooked rugs suitable for the office, den, or study. The colors and designs are strong and masculine.

PATTERN

"Rousseau's Tiger"
27 by 39 inches

MATERIALS

If you do not choose to dye, you may purchase your wool from Jane Olson (see Sources).

Tiger

1 yard total of 5 shades of rust wool, as follows:

Tail and upper rear leg. 2 ounces of dark rust wool.

Body and face. 3 ounces of medium-dark rust wool.

Thigh and upper leg. 4 ounces of medium rust wool.

Nose and foot. 2 ounces of medium-light rust wool.

Chin and chest. 1 ounce of very light rust wool.

Black stripes and outline on eyes, nose, and mouth. 1/4 yard of black wool.

Ruff and face markings. 6-by-12-inch piece of white wool.

Whiskers. Scrap of natural (off-white) wool.

Eyes. Scrap of yellow-green wool. (I used Bright Green on gold wool, but any acid green will do.)

Sky

1/2 yard of pale cream wool spot dyed with pale green.

Lotus flowers

Medium, medium-light, and very light shades of tiger rust wool.

Outline. 6-by-12-inch piece of natural (off-white) wool.

Petals. 1/3 yard of white wool.

Flower centers. Scraps of gold and medium blue wool.

Lotus stems and leaves

Stems. 4-by-12-inch piece of bright green wool.

Veins. Scraps of dark green wool.

Leaves. 1/3 yard of Dorr Sunflower gold wool spot dyed with Bronze Green.

Foreground grasses

8 pieces (6 by 12 inches) each of tweed, plaid, checks, and-solid green (3 ounces total) overdyed with Bronze Green, Dark Green, and Bright Green.

Middle ground

1/3 yard of white and beige wool overdyed with several shades of Bronze Green and Reseda Green. 6-by-12-inch piece of dark camel wool.

Background

1/2 yard of white wool overdyed with very light Bronze and Reseda Green.

Border

1/2 yard of black and white plaid or check wool overdyed with Dark Green.

One row of dark tiger rust.

DYES

(Cushing's Perfection Acid Dye)

Golden Brown

Brown Rust or natural onion skins

Orange

Bright Green

Bronze Green

Dark Green

Reseda Green

Old Gold

Yellow

Dyeing for "Rousseau's Tiger"

"Rousseau's Tiger" has a rich color scheme but uses a limited palette. Shades of deep greens in the foreground fade to cream (spot dyed with pale greens) in the sky. The deep, rich shades of rust in the tiger decrease in value to a very light rust, repeated in the lotus flowers. The border picks up the deep rust in a single row, followed by several rows of dark green, and ends with four rows of the darkest green plaid found in the foreground grasses. By repeating colors in various intensities throughout the rug, a simple color scheme becomes sophisticated through the use of overdyed patterned wools and spot dyeing.

Dyeing the Tiger

Prepare the wool the same way whether you plan to use natural onion skin dyeing or commercial dyes. Directions for both are given below.

"Rousseau's Tiger" is hooked with #8 cut. Rip the proper amounts of white wool from selvage to selvage for each of the five shades of rust, as follows. Leftover wool will be used to hook the lotus blossoms.

Dark rust
   6 inches or 2 ounces.

Medium-dark rust
   9 inches or 3 ounces.

Medium rust
   12 inches or 4 ounces.

Medium-light rust
   6 inches or 2 ounces.

Pale rust
   3 inches or 1 ounce.

Soak these wool strips in water overnight or for several hours before dyeing.

Using Natural Onion Skins. Gather your dried Golden Globe onion shells at a farmers' market or supermarket. My grocer is happy to save the skins for me. If you have a garden, save the dried skins when cleaning your onions, but no dirt, please. Onion skins last indefinitely. I save them in a mesh or paper bag as I accumulate them.

To dye the wool for this rug, you will need enough onion skins to fill a 2-gallon dyeing kettle. You can use your soup pot for this dye bath, as onion skins are not poisonous. Soak the onion skins overnight in water filled 3/4 to the top of the pot. The next day, simmer the shells for one hour to leach out the dye.

You will dye in sequence from the darkest onion skin rust to the lightest onion skin peach. You can obtain deep values with natural dyes only in the first dye bath. A longer dyeing time can darken a value just so much. Each subsequent dye bath will become lighter and lighter. I use a little salt for the first dye bath, then add white vinegar to the medium dye baths to hasten takeup and mottle the color.

The darkest rust (1) will be used for the tail and upper rear leg. Immerse the 2-ounce strip of wool in the onion skin dye pot. Stir the strip in and under the shells. Add 1 tablespoon of plain salt, and stir again. Leave this strip simmer for thirty minutes or so to obtain the darkest shade possible. Remove the wool to a separate 1-quart container of water, and set the color by adding 1/4 cup of vinegar. Simmer for fifteen minutes to be sure that the dye is fast. Cool, wash, and dry the wool.

The medium-dark rust (2) is for the body and face. To mottle the wool, add 1/2 cup of vinegar to the original dye bath, stir, and simmer. Place 3 ounces of wool in the dye bath, and stir among the shells. Simmer the wool for about ten minutes before adding the next strip.

The medium rust (3) will be used for the thigh and upper outstretched leg, which should be slightly lighter than the body to create a contrast. Simmer the 4-ounce piece of wool for twenty minutes along with the second wool strip.

The medium-light rust (4) is for the nose and foot. Before you add this 2-ounce strip, strain out the shells. This is a mess! Place a colander over another dye pot. I have a 2-quart stainless steel mixing bowl that is perfect for this step. Fish out the dyed strips, and place them in the sink so that you can carefully pick over the wool and wash off the spent shells. Then dump the shells into the colander. I let the wool strips cool for ease in handling. Use rinse water the same temperature as the wool to prevent matting. The spent shells are difficult to remove, but do a good job so that your washer will not suffer. Picking bits of shells out of the washer drum is not fun! I end up shaking the strips outside or into a wastebasket for final removal. Do not put the spent shells in the garbage disposal. I learned this the hard way and wound up with an exorbitant plumber bill. Partially drying your wool before placing it in the dryer will enable you to shake off the remaining shells. They are persistent!

Return the strained dye bath to the stove, add 1/4 cup more vinegar, and insert the fourth strip. Simmer for twenty minutes.

The very light pale rust (5) is for the chin and chest. Your dye bath should now be almost clear of color. Into this depleted dye, drop the final, 1-ounce strip. Simmer until all the rust is absorbed or until the very pale shade of rust is obtained.

Keep in mind that dyeing with natural plant materials is not foolproof. Natural dyeing takes close attention to see that the correct color is obtained. You can set the color at any step in the color takeup by simmering in a separate pan of water and vinegar, so be alert and ready to remove the wool when the desired value is achieved.

Using Commercial Dyes. If dyeing with Cushing dyes, use the open pan dyeing method.

The darkest rust (1) will be used for the tail and upper rear legs. For 2 ounces of white wool, dissolve 1/32 teaspoon of Brown Rust, 1/32 teaspoon of Golden Brown, and 1/32 teaspoon of Orange in 1 cup of boiling water. To a 1-gallon pan of water, add the dye solution and 1 teaspoon of salt, and stir. Immerse the wool, lifting once or twice to be sure that all surfaces are saturated, before returning the wool to the dye pot. Apply heat, and add 1/2 cup of vinegar when the simmer begins. This is a heavy load of dye, so it will be necessary to add another 1/2 cup of vinegar after fifteen minutes of simmering for complete takeup. Process the wool for one hour. Cool, wash, and rinse.

The medium-dark rust (2) is for the body and face. Dissolve $1/32$ teaspoon each of Brown Rust, Golden Brown, and Orange in 1 cup of boiling water. Place in a 1-gallon dye pot with 1 teaspoon of salt, and add the pre-soaked 3-ounce piece of wool. Lift the wool several times to be sure that all surfaces are saturated before dropping the wool into the dye bath. After fifteen minutes, add $1/4$ cup of vinegar. Continue to stir and add $1/2$ cup more vinegar after simmering for another fifteen minutes. Process the wool for forty-five minutes. Cool, wash, and rinse the wool.

The medium rust (3) is for the thigh and upper leg, which need to be slightly lighter to differentiate the body parts. For 4 ounces of wool, use $1/32$ teaspoon each of Brown Rust, Golden Brown, and Orange. Add 1 teaspoon of salt to a 1-gallon dye pot. Immerse the wool and bring to a simmer. Add $1/2$ cup of vinegar. Simmer for twenty minutes, and add $1/2$ cup more vinegar. Process the wool for forty-five minutes. Cool, wash, and rinse.

The medium-light rust (4) will be used for the nose and foot of the tiger. For 2 ounces of white wool, dissolve 1/64 teaspoon each of Brown Rust, Golden Brown, and Orange in 1 cup of boiling water. Reserve 1 teaspoon of this dye solution for value (5). To a 1-gallon pan of water, add the remainder of the dye solution, $1/2$ teaspoon of salt, and the 2-ounce piece of wool. Process as above for forty-five minutes, adding $1/2$ cup vinegar at simmer stage.

The very light rust (5) is for the chin and chest. Add the reserved 1 teaspoon of dye solution plus $1/2$ teaspoon of salt to a 1-quart dye pot. Into this water, add the final 1-ounce strip. Saturate the wool, and bring to a simmer. After fifteen minutes, add $1/4$ cup of vinegar to complete the takeup. Continue to process the wool until the dye bath is clear. Cool, wash, and rinse the wool.

In all cases throughout this commercial dyeing process, be sure that your values range from dark to very pale.

Dyeing the Sky

Dye 1/2 yard of white wool the palest Old Gold. Dissolve 1/64 teaspoon Old Gold in 1 cup of boiling water. Add 1/2 teaspoon of salt to a 1-gallon dye pot of water. Immerse the presoaked wool into the dye bath, and lift once or twice to fully expose the wool to the color. Because this is such a light color, wait a few minutes before adding 1/4 cup of vinegar to the dye bath. Lift the wool on a strong fork, splash in the vinegar, stir around, and return the wool for thirty minutes or until takeup is complete. Add more vinegar if needed. You will be spot dyeing the sky, so longer simmering is not needed at this time. When the dye is absorbed, place the wool in the washer, spin out the water, and allow it to cool for ease in handling.

In the meantime, prepare a very weak dye for spot dyeing. You want just a glimmer of green in the sky. Place several grains (half of 1/128 teaspoon) of Dark Green in 1/2 cup of boiling water plus 1/4 cup of vinegar. Be sure this dye is dissolved. Repeat this procedure for solutions of Bronze Green and Bright Green. Remember, these solutions are barely there. By now, your sky wool is spun out and cool enough to handle. Do not rinse.

You will now casserole dye the sky wool. Fold the wool in half (9 inches) and lay it in accordion pleats that run the length of the fabric. Place the pleated fabric in a casserole pan lined with aluminum foil. Now carefully pour the extremely light dye solutions from side to side across the folded cream wool, alternating bands of color. You may not use all of the dye solution. Leave stripes of cream fabric free of green tint between the different colors. Cover the casserole with foil, and steam the wool for thirty minutes on top of the stove. Cool, wash, and dry the wool.

Dyeing the Lotus Flowers

You have already dyed the shades of rust for the flowers, when you dyed the tiger wool. Off-white or beige for the white petal outline can be purchased. One gold strip will be enough for the band on the lotus center. For the centers, use a scrap of any available medium blue wool.

Dyeing the Serrated Leaves

The lotus leaves are Dorr Sunflower gold, spot dyed with Bronze Green. To spot dye the gold wool, presoak it in wetting agent. Spin it out in the washer, but do not rinse it. Now arrange the gold wool in a 1-gallon dye pot in many folds. Push the wool down, then draw up many little "puffs" to receive the Bronze Green for spot dyeing.

Dissolve $1/32$ teaspoon Bronze Green in 1 cup of boiling water. Stir thoroughly to be sure that the dye is totally dissolved. Add $1/4$ cup of vinegar to the dye solution. Drip the strong Bronze Green dye on the little "puffs" in *very* small spots for a speckled, not diffused, appearance. This takes patience. A glass eyedropper is useful here, but throw it out afterward, as it will be contaminated! After dribbling on the Bronze Green dye, carefully add a scant $1/4$ to $1/2$ cup of water to the bottom, lifting the wool before pouring it in. Do not pour the water directly on the wool, or you may disturb your spots. Cover the pan with foil and process the wool for thirty minutes. Cool, wash, and dry.

Dyeing the Lotus Stems and Tiger Eyes

Five strands of Bright Green are needed for the lotus stems. Dye a sufficient amount of white scraps with $1/64$ teaspoon Bright Green in 1 cup of boiling water. Use a 1-quart dye pot. Add a sprinkle of salt and 1 teaspoon of vinegar before simmering for thirty minutes.

This same dye solution can be used to dye one strip of Sunflower gold to produce the yellow-green needed for the tiger's eyes.

Dyeing the Foreground Grasses and Leaf Veins

To achieve a variety of grasses, I use six different plaids, checks, tweeds, and solids overdyed with Dark Green, Bronze Green, and, on the darker fabrics, Bright Green. This section takes 3 ounces of combined wools. I use all my old scraps of the above materials, overdyeing them in three different small dye pots. For each dye solution, use 2/32 teaspoon of the dye, 1/2 cup of vinegar, and 1 teaspoon of salt in 1 quart of water. You can also use some of the border dark green plaid and the dark green inner border wool when hooking this area. Be sure that the grasses are darker than the middle ground, or they will disappear. Use some of the dark green wool for leaf veins.

Dyeing the Middle Ground

The middle ground is a combination of Bronze Green and Reseda Green, spot dyed with Dark Green. Use 4 ounces of white wool or a combination of white and beige wools for more variety. Dissolve 2/32 teaspoon Bronze Green and 1/32 teaspoon Reseda Green in 1 cup of boiling water. Add the dye solution and 2 teaspoons of salt to a 2-gallon dye pot filled halfway with water. Immerse the wool. Stir and lift the wool until it is saturated with dye. Then apply heat. After fifteen minutes, add 1/2 cup of vinegar, and simmer thirty to forty-five minutes, stirring often until takeup is complete. Allow the fabric to cool, and squeeze out the dye bath in the sink. Do not rinse. Inspect the wool for any light spots. Rearrange the wool back in the dye vessel by scrunching it down in a crowded fashion. Pull any overly light spots to the top to receive the Dark Green spot dyeing. If you have included beige wool in the dye bath, put this darker material on the bottom so that it will absorb less of the Dark Green solution. Add 1 cup of water to the pot, if needed, for the next step.

Prepare the Dark Green top dressing as you have done before when spot dyeing the sky. Add 1/64 teaspoon Dark Green dye to 1 cup of boiling water. Stir to be sure that the dye is totally dissolved. You will dribble this weak solution on top of your scrunched fabric. You want this dye to dissipate into the green material so that it blends. Have a glass of water standing by to dilute the spot if too much spills on any one area. Steam the wool for another thirty minutes to set the spots. Cool, wash, and dry the wool.

Dyeing the Background

You want the middle ground and background areas to blend, but not match. To give a lighter appearance, dissolve 1/32 teaspoon Bronze Green and 1/32 teaspoon Reseda Green plus 1 teaspoon of salt in 1 cup of boiling water. Add the dye solution to a 1-gallon dye pot. Immerse the wool. Lift and stir the wool in the dye bath. Add 1/2 cup of vinegar after simmering for fifteen more minutes. Continue to process the wool until the dye bath is exhausted. Cool, wash, and dry the wool.

Dyeing the Border

The border is dyed a very dark Dark Green on a black and white plaid. A very strong dye solution is required. Use 3/4 teaspoon Dark Green plus 1/32 teaspoon Yellow for 6 ounces of plaid wool. Before presoaking, rip off one-third (or 2 ounces) of the border material. This smaller piece will be dyed for a slightly lighter inner border (two rows). Dissolve the dye in 1 cup of boiling water. Reserve 1/4 cup of the dye solution for dyeing the inner border.

In a 1-gallon dye pot, stir the dye bath until the dark dye is completely incorporated. Add 1 tablespoon of salt. Wait to add the vinegar. Immerse the presoaked 4 ounces of border wool in the dye bath, lifting and stirring to be sure that all surfaces are saturated. Until you add the vinegar, the Dark Green dye will not completely take up, so simmer this initial dye bath for about ten minutes before adding 1/2 cup of vinegar. Add the 1/2 cup of vinegar with one hand while lifting the fabric out of the dye bath with a strong fork. Swirl around the vinegar before returning the wool to the dye bath. Are you getting good at this? The addition of 1/2 cup more vinegar every fifteen minutes will complete the takeup. Process for thirty to forty-five minutes. Permit the wool to cool in the dye bath.

Using the reserved 1/4 cup of dye solution from the outer border, dye the inner border (2 ounces) in the same manner as above.

Hooking "Rousseau's Tiger"

Most of the wool for "Rousseau's Tiger" is #8 cut. Use #6 cut for the tiger's face where indicated.

Hooking the Tiger's Head

Begin with the eyes. Cut the green eyes, black outline and pupil, and white dot with a #4 or #6 cutting blade. These are very small areas. Outline the eyes with black. Fill in the green eyes, leaving a small space in the center of each for the black pupil and white dot. Add each pupil (2 loops), and place the white dot (1 loop) under the black.

Using (4) rust wool, hook in the nose. Under the nose, hook one row of black, the dividing line, and the mouth. The #6 cut whiskers are next. Using the off-white wool, hook three lines of whiskers on either side, drooping them out into the ruff. Hook several short black lines (#6 cut) between the whiskers to define the muzzle.

Fill in the area on either side of the nose with (3) rust wool. Hook the black stripes on the head. Outline the eyes with one row of white, running this white strip up over the eyes between the black bands.

Hook the chin area with (5) rust wool. Finish the head with (2) rust wool, and outline the ears with one row. You are now ready to hook the white ruff around the tiger's head. I used #8 cut, but with #6 it will be easier to obtain a shaggy, furry look. Beginning inside the ears, hook the ruff in points, out and in, all around the face. You will have to go around the off-white whiskers, which should show up against the white fur.

Finish the head, hooking the ears. You have already outlined them and placed some white fur inside. Now make one row beside the outline with (3) rust wool, and complete the inner ear with (4) rust wool. If you are using #6 cut for the inner ear, you may have space for one row of (5) rust around the white fur inside the ear.

Hooking the Tiger's Body

Begin the body by hooking in all the black stripes. Hook in (5) rust wool under the chin, completing the chest.

Hook the tail, upper rear leg, and upper neck with (1) rust wool. Hook the pad of the foot with black spots, and fill in with (4) rust wool.

The thigh and upper extended leg are hooked in (3) rust wool. Hook the claws in black with #6 cut wool.

Now complete the tiger body with (2) rust wool. This color should be worked into the tail and thigh for a smooth transition. Hook the lower rear leg in (2) rust wool as well.

Hooking the Lotus Flowers and Leaves

The lotus blossoms have large white petals outlined in off-white. One row of gold outlines the blue flower center. Outline all the upper petals in (4) rust wool, filling in the forward petals in (5) rust wool and the rear petals and bud in (3) rust wool.

Then hook one row of bright green for the stems and one row of dark green for the leaf veins.

Choose the brightest gold strips for the leaf outlines. Heavily spotted strips may disappear into the middle ground. Outline with a serrated edge by hooking out two loops, in two loops, and up two loops. Fill in the rest of the leaf with the speckled material.

Hooking the Field and the Border

Before you begin the background field, you must first stabilize the edges to keep the rug from distorting and maintain the rectangle. Hook one row of (1) rust wool all around the inner border, then hook the inner border (two rows) and finish the outer border (four rows). Number your grasses from one to eight, and intermingle shades of Dark Green, Bright Green, and Bronze Green overdyed fabrics. Hook up to a point and down again or vice versa; avoid a line of cuts at the bottom of the rug at the same place. Don't forget to put your initials in a lower corner with a lighter green.

Hooking the Middle Ground

Outline all shapes in the middle ground with your darkest shade of Bronze Green, then fill in. Hook horizontally, varying the shades of color. The camel band of ground is also hooked at this time.

Hooking the Background

Outline the shapes in the background, taking particular care to hook the grasses on the horizon in points as you did the foreground grasses. Hook horizontally and complete this area.

Hooking the Sky

Outline the sky around the shapes and the inside border, then hook horizontally to complete the area.

PATTERN

"Mallard Decoys"

33 by 25 inches

MATERIALS

Drakes

Heads. 1 ounce of dark green wool.

Neck rings, tail feathers, and wing speculums. 1/2 ounce of white wool.

Tails, tail curls, and nostrils. 1/2 ounce of black wool.

Breasts and eyes. 1 ounce of chestnut brown wool. Scraps of light and dark gray tweed from female duck material overdyed light chestnut brown.

Speculums. Scrap of dark blue-purple wool.

Backs. Scrap of dark brown wool.

Bills. 1/4 ounce (3-by-12-inch strip) of deep gold wool.

Bodies and wings. 3 ounces of white wool dyed silver gray (28 1/2 by 18 inches).

Ducks

Throats, chins, tails, and body outlines. 1 ounce of light chestnut wool.

Bodies. 3 ounces of light, medium, and dark gray tweeds dyed a variety of chestnut.

Backs. 1 ounce of medium chestnut brown wool.

Bills. 1/4 ounce (3-by-12-inch strip) of medium rusty orange wool.

Eyes and nostrils. Scrap of black wool.

Background

12 ounces (1 yard) of dove gray wool overdyed with Silver Gray Green.

Border

4 ounces of dark green wool.

2 ounces of chestnut brown wool.

1 ounce of light chestnut brown wool.

1 ounce of dark brown wool.

DYES

(Cushing's Perfection Acid Dye)

Silver Gray Green

Dark Green

Silver Gray

Dark Brown

Golden Brown

*"Four Ducks," floating
in a sparkling pool of
dark blue wool, is a
domesticated version
of "Mallard Decoys."*

Dyeing "Mallard Decoys"

Similar colors are used for the male and female mallards; these same colors are carried out into the border. For this reason, and to simplify dyeing, the dye formulas given are for the combined amounts. I used #8 cut for the entire rug. If using #8 cut, you may tear the wool from selvage to selvage. But tear tweeds with the selvage, as they are loosely woven. Tweeds are important here to simulate feathers.

Dyeing the Dark Green

Presoak 5 ounces of white wool. Dissolve 1 teaspoon Dark Green in 1 cup of boiling water. Add 1 tablespoon of salt. In a 2-gallon dye pot, add the dye solution and immerse the presoaked wool. Lift and lower to fully saturate the fibers with dye. Using the open pan dyeing method, gradually apply heat. At the simmer stage, add the first 1/4 cup of vinegar. Add 1/4 cup more vinegar every fifteen minutes of processing for 1 hour. Work the wool well to avoid unwanted blotches. If the dye bath is not exhausted, add more vinegar and heat. Cool in the dye pot.

Dyeing the Chestnut Brown

Presoak 4 ounces of white wool. Dissolve 1/4 teaspoon Dark Brown and 2/32 teaspoon Golden Brown in 1 cup of boiling water. Add 1 tablespoon of salt. Using a 2-gallon dye pot, process with open pan dyeing as above.

For medium chestnut brown, presoak 1 ounce of white wool. Dissolve 3/64 teaspoon Dark Brown and 1/64 teaspoon Golden Brown in 1 cup of boiling water. Add 1 teaspoon of salt. Using the open pan dyeing method, add 1/4 cup of vinegar at the simmer stage, and another 1/4 cup after 1/2 hour. Process until takeup is complete. Cool in the dye pot.

For light chestnut brown, presoak 2 ounces of white wool. Dissolve 2/32 teaspoon Dark Brown, 1/64 teaspoon Golden Brown, plus 1 teaspoon of salt. Process with the open pan dyeing method as above.

Dyeing the Gray Tweeds

You will need a mixture of light, medium, and dark gray tweeds to simulate feathers. Presoak 1 ounce of each. Dissolve 4/32 teaspoon Dark Brown, 1/32 teaspoon Golden Brown, plus 2 teaspoons of salt. Dye all three shades of tweed in this dye solution with the open pan dyeing method as above.

Dyeing the Silver Gray

You will dip dye a 28 1/2-by-18-inch piece of white wool (3 ounces) in three values of very light Silver Gray. Dissolve 1/128 teaspoon Silver Gray in 1 cup of boiling water. Pour one-third of this dye solution into a 1-gallon dye bath filled about half full. Add 1 teaspoon of salt. Immerse the entire piece, lifting and lowering it until it is thoroughly saturated with the dye. Bring to a simmer, and add 2 tablespoons of vinegar. Continue to process until the dye bath is clear. This is your lightest shade of silver gray. Now, wearing rubber gloves, lift the piece by one 18-inch side, and prepare to dip dye two-thirds of the piece.

Add the next $1/3$ cup of dye solution to the dye bath. Lift and lower the wool two-thirds deep into the dye bath. Add 2 tablespoons more vinegar and process, lifting and lowering the piece until the dye bath is clear. Remove the wool, adding the last $1/3$ cup of Silver Gray solution. Add 2 more tablespoons of vinegar. Now reimmerse the piece for the last and darkest one-third section of silver gray. When this dye bath is exhausted, slump the wool in one corner, and steam for fifteen minutes. Cool in the dye bath, wash, and rinse.

Dyeing the Background

Presoak 1 yard of dove gray wool. You will overdye this color with a tint of Silver Gray Green, then spot dye it as well. Dissolve $2/32$ teaspoon of Silver Gray Green with 1 teaspoon of salt. Add the dye solution to a 2-gallon dye bath. Thoroughly saturate the gray wool before adding heat. Process with the open pan dyeing method, adding $1/4$ cup of vinegar after fifteen minutes and another after thirty minutes. Process for forty-five minutes. Cool in the dye pot.

Dissolve separately $1/64$ teaspoon Silver Gray and $1/64$ teaspoon Silver Gray Green each in 1 cup of boiling water. Add $1/2$ teaspoon of salt and $1/4$ cup of vinegar to each cup. You will use this dye to spot dye the background wool. Pour out half of the background dye bath. Rearrange the wool in hills and valleys, puckering the wool in the dye bath. Drip Silver Gray dye solution into the valleys, and drip Silver Gray Green dye solution on the tops of the hills. If the spots look too dark, dilute the solutions further. I keep a glass of water standing by to diffuse dark spots. Don't use much water, though, or the dye will bleed into the background and become indistinct. Do not disturb this spot dyeing. Continue to simmer for thirty more minutes, cool in the dye pot, wash, and dry.

Hooking "Mallard Decoys"

Hooking the Drakes

Because of overlapping, it is easier to hook the rear drake after finishing the ducks, so begin by hooking the front mallard drake. Hook its chestnut eye, black nostril, and gold bill. Hook the white neck ring, then fill in the green head. Frame the speculum in one row of white, and add the violet. Hook the lower wing on either side of the speculum in gray tweed overdyed with chestnut. The wing above the speculum graduates in shades of chestnut brown, from dark to medium to overdyed light gray tweed. Fill in the dark chestnut brown breast and one row of dark brown across the back.

The black and white tail feathers are hooked next. The body is lighter below than above. Hook the lightest shade of silver gray at the bottom edge, then gradually add the middle value as you swing around the wing to hook the upper wing.

Hooking the Ducks

Start hooking the ducks with their black eyes, nostrils, and orange bills. Outline the heads and wings with the darkest overdyed gray tweed. Now add the light chestnut throats and tail feathers, outlining the ducks' breasts and bellies. The heads, breasts, and backs are hooked in alternate shades of medium chestnut brown and the light and medium chestnut-overdyed gray tweeds. Hook following the contours of the ducks, curving down the necks and around the breasts.

Outline the wing feathers with all shades from dark to light chestnut to define their shapes. Finish the wing tips with the same assortment of chestnut-dyed tweeds used for the breasts and backs.

Hooking the Border

To stabilize your edges, hook the border before beginning the background. The rows are as follows: one row of dark green, two light chestnut, one dark chestnut, two medium chestnut, one dark brown, two silver gray green, and four dark green to finish.

Hooking the Background

First outline the border edges and all the decoys, then begin filling in the background with wavy lines. Add your initials, and the date if you wish, in one of the chestnut browns. Keep your waves relatively calm. The mottling will take care of surface interest. Hook horizontally, and float around the decoys, turning and burying the cut ends somewhere in the "pond," not at the edges. Learn to turn and reverse the direction of your rows to avoid a distressing pileup of cuts along an edge.

PATTERN ———————————————————————————————

"Horse Portrait—Diamond Lil"

2 by 3 feet

Courtesy of Barbara Pirtle

MATERIALS

If you do not care to dye, wool for the horse head and bridle can be purchased from Maryanne Lincoln, Sand (N38), 12-by-12-inch sheets of each 6 values.

Horse

Nose. 1/4 ounce (3 by 14 inches) of taupe wool *or* White Sand (deepest value), Maryanne Lincoln "Country Colors."
Mane. 1/2 ounce of checks and plaids overdyed dark brown.
Blaze and eye. 1/4 ounce of white wool.
Head. 2 ounces of 3 shades of medium brown wool.
Eye outline and pupil highlight. Scrap of black and white check wool.
Nostril, mouth, and eye. Scrap of black wool.

Bridle

1/2 ounce of lightest brown, tan, or beige wool.
Ring. Scrap of gold wool.

Diamond center

9 ounces of cream wool.

Corners

Flower centers. 1/4 ounce of gold wool.
Flowers and cherries. 1 ounce each of light, medium-dark, and dark terra cotta wool *or* three 8-value 3-by-12-inch swatches of Sturbridge Red (R12-6T).
Flowers and border line. 3 ounces of medium terra cotta wool *or* one sheet 12-by-24-inches of value #4 Sturbridge Red, Maryanne Lincoln "Country Colors."
Stems. 1 ounce of camel wool *or* remaining browns from horse swatches.
Leaves. 4 ounces of 3 shades of medium green wool *or* three 6-value 3-by-12 inch swatches of Forest Green, Maryanne Lincoln "Country Colors."
Veins. 3-by-18-inch piece of dark maroon plaid *or* use darkest value of Sturbridge Red swatch.

Background

9 ounces of dark green wool.

Border

Medium terra cotta wool, cream wool, and dark green wool drawn from the wool used for the diamond center, corners, and background.

DYES

(Cushing's Perfection Acid Dye)

Dark Green

Old Gold

Reseda Green

Dark Brown

Golden Brown

Terra Cotta

Tearing the Wool

I used #8 cut for the entire rug; if you do so, you may tear the wool from selvage to selvage. If you plan to use a finer cut, tear the wool with the selvage. To do this, tear a quarter yard (18 by 28½ inch) piece of white wool into four 7-by-18-inch strips to dye the horse and bridle.

For the border line and flowers, tear ½ yard into nine 3-by-18-inch pieces with the selvage. Leave the remaining 18-by-30 inch piece untorn. For the leaves, tear a quarter yard piece, 18-by-28½ inches, into nine strips. You will use three 3-by-18 inch pieces for each of the three shades of green.

Dyeing for "Horse Portrait—Diamond Lil"

Dyeing the Horse

Make a dye solution of 4/32 teaspoon Dark Brown and 2/32 teaspoon Golden Brown in 2 cups of boiling water to dissolve the dye for the basic color of Diamond Lil. This will be used in varying strengths to dye the shades of brown for the coat and bridle. Reserve 1 tablespoon of the dye solution for dyeing the bridle.

Presoak the four 7-by-18-inch strips. Pour 1 cup of the dye solution with 2 teaspoons of salt into a 1-gallon dye pot. You will dye one of the strips in this dye bath to obtain the darkest shade of horse brown.

Immerse the strip, thoroughly saturating the wool, and bring to a simmer. Add ¼ cup of vinegar, and continue to work the wool. After fifteen more minutes, add another ¼ cup of vinegar, and continue to process the wool with open pan dyeing for 1 hour. Cool, but do not wash the wool.

To pan two, add 1 teaspoon of salt and ⅔ cup of the dye solution. Proceed to dye the second strip with the open pan dyeing method as above for the medium shade of horse brown.

To pan three, add 1 teaspoon of salt and ⅓ cup of the dye solution, and process the third strip of wool as above for the lightest shade of horse brown.

To pan four, add the reserved 1 tablespoon of dye solution and 1/2 teaspoon of salt to dye the bridle strip. Process as above. Wait to wash the horse browns until you dye the mane.

Dyeing the Mane

Presoak 1/2 ounce of white, black and white plaid, or dark gray tweed scraps. Dissolve 4/32 teaspoon Dark Brown dye with 1 tablespoon of salt in 1 cup of boiling water. Immerse the scraps and thoroughly work them to saturate the fibers before applying heat. Add 1/4 cup of vinegar at the simmer stage and another 1/4 cup fifteen minutes later. This is a heavy load of dye and may need more vinegar later in the dyeing process.

At this time, analyze your horse browns. Do they need spot dyeing? If so, splatter some of the depleted dark brown dye on those that do, and steam these wools for fifteen minutes to set the dye. When all the browns are dyed, wash, rinse, and dry the wool.

Dyeing the Diamond Center

Presoak 9 ounces (3/4 yard) of white wool. Dissolve 1/32 teaspoon of Old Gold and 1 teaspoon of salt in 1 cup of boiling water. Add the dye solution to a 2-gallon dye pot filled 3/4 full of water. Immerse the wool and work well, adding 1/4 cup of vinegar at the simmer stage and stirring well. Lift and lower the wool to saturate all the surfaces with the dye, and simmer for thirty minutes. Cool, wash, and dry the wool.

Dyeing the Background

Dissolve 2 teaspoons Dark Green dye in 1 cup of boiling water. Add the dye solution plus 1 tablespoon of salt to a 2-gallon dye pot filled 3/4 full of water. Drop in the 9-ounce presoaked piece of white wool, lifting and lowering several times to be sure all the surfaces are saturated. Wait ten minutes, then lift the wool out of the dye bath, add the first 1/2 cup of vinegar, stir, and lower the wool again, being sure to open up the wool to the dye. Simmer for ten more minutes, and add another

1/2 cup of vinegar, lifting and stirring as before. Continue to simmer for fifteen more minutes and add 1/2 cup more vinegar. By adding vinegar gradually, you will avoid harsh dark spots on your wool and ensure takeup. Process for one hour using open pan dyeing. Cool in the dye bath, wash, and dry.

Dyeing the Terra Cotta Flowers and Border Line

Presoak the nine 3-by-18-inch and 18-by-30-inch pieces of wool. Dissolve 4/32 teaspoon Terra Cotta and 1 tablespoon of salt in 1 cup of boiling water for three dark strips in pan one. If you are overdyeing a green plaid with Terra Cotta for veins, substitute this 3-by-18-inch strip for one of the white ones when dyeing those strips in pan one.

Dissolve 1/32 teaspoon Terra Cotta and 1 teaspoon of salt in pan two for three strips for the medium flowers.

Dissolve 1/64 teaspoon Terra Cotta, and 1 teaspoon of salt in pan three for three strips for the light flowers.

In a larger dye pot, dissolve 6/32 teaspoon Terra Cotta and 1 tablespoon of salt for the 18-by-30-inch piece to be used for the medium-dark flowers and border row.

Process this wool with the open pan dyeing method, adding 1/4 cup of vinegar at the simmer stage and another 1/4 cup of vinegar after thirty minutes during the one-hour dyeing period. If the dye has not taken up after forty-five minutes, add 1/4 cup more vinegar. Cool, wash, and dry.

Dyeing the Leaves

You will use three 3-by-18-inch pieces for each of three shades of green, using the graduated strip dyeing method. Presoak the wool

Dissolve 3/32 teaspoon Reseda Green in 1 cup of boiling water with 1 tablespoon of salt.

In pan one, place 1/2 cup of the dye solution. Refill the cup with water, and place 1/2 cup of dye solution in pan two. Again refill the cup with water, and place 1/2 cup of the dye solution in pan three. Spot dye with the remaining dye solution or discard. Place 3 presoaked strips in each pan and work the wool. Add 1/4 cup of vinegar to each pan at simmer. Add another $1/4$ cup of vinegar after thirty minutes. Process for one hour, and cool in the dye bath. Wash, rinse, and dry.

Hooking "Horse Portrait—Diamond Lil"

Hooking the Horse
I cut all my wool with #8 cut, which fits the pattern lines. If you plan to use a smaller cut, adjust the spaces for the different widths. Cut all the shades of medium brown. You will mix these colors when hooking the horse head. Hook the eye with a black and white check outline, a black center, a white eyeball, and one loop of check for a highlight. Trim this highlight scrap into #6 cut. Hook the mouth and nostril with black. Hook the nose with taupe. Using the dark mane brown, hook the forelock and ear folds. Add the white blaze. Hook the gold ring and the bridle.

You are now ready to hook the mane with several shades of dark brown. Hook vertically, as the mane would naturally fall, alternating the various shades. Vary the location of the cut ends so that they do not all occur at the edges. Begin hooking the horse highlights with the lightest shade of medium brown, moving down the nose and filling in the cheek. Hook the head with medium brown, saving the darkest shade for the area touching the cream background, behind the bridle, and down the neck. Hook one row of medium brown above the reins before vertically hooking the neck with various shades of medium brown. Use the lightest shade in the center of the neck to indicate a shiny coat and under the center mane to distinguish the fall of the mane from the horse's neck.

Hooking the Diamond Center
Outline the horse and the diamond center with one or two rows of background cream. This is essential to maintain the shapes. Then, in an undulating fashion, hook vertically from one side to the other.

Hooking the Border

To maintain the rectangle, hook in the border rows, starting with an inner row of cream, then one row of medium terra cotta, and three rows of dark green on the outer edge of the rug.

Hooking the Flowers

The flowers are centered in gold. Use three shades of Terra Cotta—light, medium, and medium dark. Outline each flower in a contrasting red. Hook the cherries in dark red, using some of this shade to outline the deepest flower. Now hook in the camel stems and the dark veins. Alternate the three shades of medium green for the leaves.

Hooking the Corner Background

Use dark green to outline the border rows, the diamond center, and all the flowers, leaves, and stems before filling in the spaces. Hook the background by contouring around the objects until you must flatten out your rows to join with the straight lines of the center and border.

Hemming Your Rug

Your rug is finished and is now ready to be hemmed. The foundation edges must be handled carefully so that they do not unravel during the binding process.

You will need the following for hemming your rug: binding yarn, cotton rug tape, a crewel or yarn needle, a large-eyed sharp needle, sharp scissors, straight pins with china heads or T-pins, and buttonhole twist or dual-purpose thread to match your wool yarn and tape.

Binding Yarn

I prefer to use a binding of wool yarn. This can be crewel wool or a knitting worsted weight yarn (four-ply). Crewel wool is beautiful and comes in many colors or may be dyed along with your border material to match. This weight yarn takes up ten times the perimeter of your rug. Several ounces will bind a 2-by-3-foot rug.

If you do not choose to dye or spend the money for crewel yarn, knitting worsted (four-ply) is an excellent choice of yarn for binding. I was lucky enough to buy pounds of wool carpet yarn from a junkyard dealer years ago when carpets were still woven with wool. This is perfect binding yarn, but knitting worsted works every bit as well and has the added strength of synthetic yarns. Be careful that the yarn does not shine; some synthetics do. I use olefin 75 percent and acrylic 25 percent yarn which comes in many colors and is inexpensive.

Rug Tape

Use cotton rug tape to finish binding your rug. It comes in many colors and can be ordered by the yard from rug suppliers (see Sources). Buy more tape than the perimeter of your finished rug. Binding shrinks and runs, so be sure to wash and iron it before sewing it onto your hem.

Acid dyes will not dye cotton. In the past, using union dyes, I was able to dye my rug tape with the border material. No more! Cushing & Co. will soon have dyes for plant fibers on the market. These new dyes will enable you to dye your own cotton rug tape to match your rug.

Tightly woven cotton fabric strips can be substituted if you cannot find the appropriate rug tape color. Burlap edges must be covered to prevent wear and fraying. Iron-on rug tape is not acceptable.

If you are using linen or cotton rug foundation, you may turn over the edges and double the fabric, to serve as a finished hem. Doubling under the foundation material will prevent fraying. This is not a perfect finishing technique, and will not take the wear as well as rug tape, but it can pass in a rug placed in low-traffic areas.

Pressing Your Rug

Before binding, press the finished rug with a damp cloth (not a commercial pressing cloth) and hot iron. The wet cloth will create steam when ironed on top of the rug face. I use a piece of an old cotton sheet. Never use a steam iron directly on the wool face. Use slight pressure and lots of steam. Keep wetting the pressing cloth, wringing out the excess water, and steam press the whole top face of the rug. This will smooth out uneven loops (if there are any) and flatten the rug for smooth binding. Permit the rug to dry flat on the floor before proceeding.

Cutting the Excess Foundation

Lay the pressed rug facedown on a counter or table so that it is completely flat. Fold over the remaining foundation edge until it is 1/4 inch from the edge of the last row of hooked loops. Pin the hem in place with china-headed pins or T-pins. Dressmaker pins sometimes get lost in the hem. The 1/4-inch folded edge will be bound with yarn.

You may cut off the excess foundation to within 1 1/4 inch of the folded edge now or wait until the rug is bound with yarn. It is easier to miter the rug corners when the excess foundation is removed, but if you are worried about the cut edge unraveling, wait to trim until later.

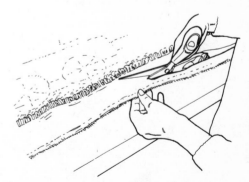

Cut off the excess foundation 1 1/4 inches from the last row of loops. This edge will be turned back and covered with cotton rug tape.

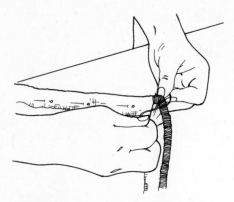

Overcast the folded 1/4-inch edge of the rug with yarn to ensure a strong binding around the perimeter of the rug. This will protect your rug from unraveling at the edges.

Binding the Rug

Thread the yarn needle with a length of yarn comfortable for you to pull through the foundation. I cut mine about 18 inches long. Begin on a side by running the yarn through the hem before starting to overcast the edge. I leave a 3-inch unknotted end to tie in later. Work from the back of the rug.

Begin to overcast the 1/4-inch foundation fold at the outer edge of your rug in the middle of one side. Work one overcast stitch directly against the other so that no foundation is visible. Continue overcasting until you run out of yarn. End by running the yarn into the foundation hem. Rethread your needle and make several running stitches along the hem to the loose end. Knot this yarn to the new length in a square knot that will be hidden in the hem before running your needle back up to the edge and continuing to overcast. Use this knotting procedure for each new length of yarn and finish by knotting in the first end with the last thread. Keep the knots away from the overcast edge so that they will not show, but will be hidden by the rug tape.

Adding Macramé Fringe

To add macramé fringe, finish the two horizontal sides with overcast yarn as described above, but do not bind the two vertical ends.

Cut lengths of yarn 12 inches long (6 inches doubled) in one or more colors to match your rug and the bound edges. This will produce a 3- to 4-inch finished fringe. Fold the yarn lengths in half, devising a color plan if using more than one color of fringe. Thread the doubled end of yarn (a loop) through the eye of a large-eyed needle. With the needle, draw this loop, keeping the yarn doubled, through the base of the 1/4-inch exposed folded-over edge of the foundation. Now bring the two loose ends down through the loop. Pull and tighten the knot against the foundation edge. You have now made a lark's head knot, covering the 1/4-inch folded-over edge. Repeat this procedure until the entire side of the rug is filled with touching lark's head knots, in a number divisible by four. This will look like your bound edge, with hanging tails.

Working in units of four, take the first and fourth strands and make a square knot over the two center strands. Repeat this procedure knotting loosely, across the end of the rug. Now, skipping the first two strands, make a series of square knots (using four strands as before) for another row; knot loosely, and leave a space between rows. You will end the second row with two strands unknotted. Repeat row one, incorporating all the strands. Trim the fringe to an even length.

Consult a book on macramé for more extensive knotting using longer lengths.

Sewing the Rug Tape

Having completed the yarn binding, you are ready to add the cotton rug tape. Cut off the excess foundation 1¼ inch from the edge that is pinned into place, if you have not already done so.

Starting at the corner, begin to stitch the cotton rug tape to the newly bound yarn edge with buttonhole twist or heavy-duty thread to match. Use a blind stitch, and keep the stitches close to each other and to the yarn-bound edge so that no foundation is visible.

Stitch around the entire rug, mitering each corner. Be sure the foundation in each corner is folded so that it will not be unduly bulky under the tape. Under no circumstances should you trim all this corner fabric away. Corners take hard wear, and burlap unravels easily, as does linen and cotton rug base.

At the last corner, overlap the cotton tape and fold back the raw edge.

Now sew down the inside edge of the rug tape to the back of the rug. You will catch a scant edge of the rug tape as you stitch the tape to the backs of the loops. Be sure not to pull these loops or dig too deeply with your needle, or the stitch will show on the face of the rug.

To complete your beautiful hooked rug, sew a name tag onto the cotton rug tape for identification in future years.

Miter the corners when adding cotton rug tape. You will catch both the foundation hem and the cotton tape when sewing around the inside edges.

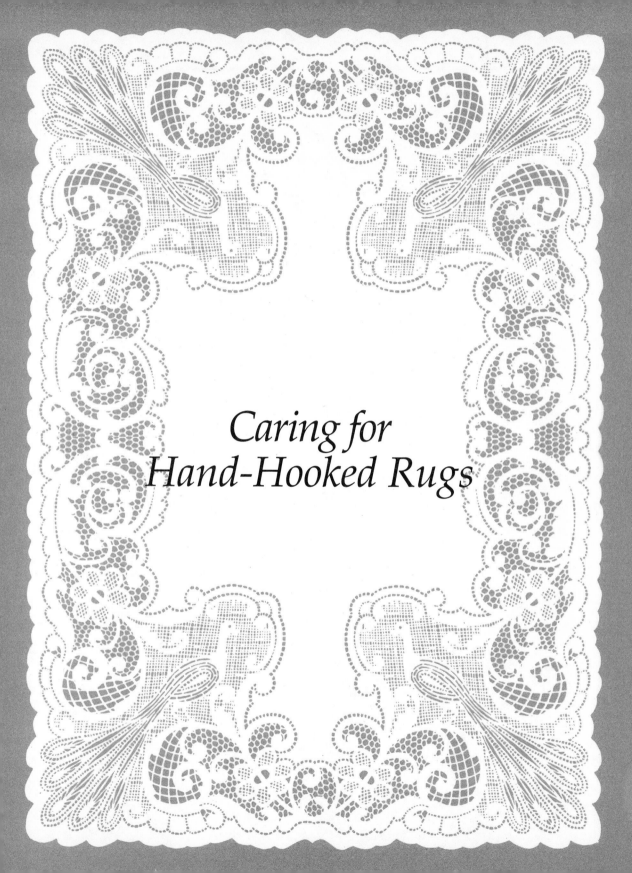

Caring for Hand-Hooked Rugs

Displaying Your Rug

The rugs in this book were created to be used on the floor. If, however, you wish to hang a hand-hooked rug, you have several options.

I previously advocated sewing Velcro strips onto the cotton rug tape binding the edges to hang a rug. I no longer recommend the use of Velcro, however, because research with quilts stored for eight years has shown that Velcro rots the cotton backing.

You can sew a sleeve of rug tape to the top of the finished rug so that it covers the binding at that edge, and insert a 3/8-inch dowel rod for hanging. Use cup hooks or curtain hardware to hang the rod from the wall.

Quilt holders made of quality hardwood hang quilts and rugs alike by pressure. There are many sizes available (see Sources).

Large rugs must be supported by a lining with strap hanging loops to eliminate stress and strain on the foundation and top of the rug. Plan to line the rug completely with tightly woven cotton. Sew a number of 1- to 2-inch twill tapes onto the cotton backing material from the bottom edge to the top edge (using the sewing machine) to loop over the hanging rod cafe curtain style. These tapes will support the entire body of the rug from bottom to top. Sleeves evenly distribute the weight but leave the stress on the top edge. Tape loops starting at the bottom of the rug will distribute the stress evenly. Blind stitch the lining to the rug, using small stitches between the yarn binding and the cotton rug tape.

If you prefer to keep these tapes invisible, leave a small area unsewn at the top of the rug, similar to a sleeve, when sewing on the twill tapes. This will accommodate a dowel rod.

Underlays for Your Rug

If you are using a hooked rug on the floor, use a rug pad underneath it. Not only does it prevent slipping on hardwood floors or wall-to-wall carpeting, but it increases the rug's durability. A 1/4-inch foam rubber pad will hold a hooked rug on the floor. Rug-Grip, a pebbly surfaced rug pad, will prevent a hooked rug from "creeping" on carpeted floors. Hooked rug suppliers provide Rug-Hold, an underlay suitable for smooth surfaces as well as carpeting.

Avoid at all costs a latex paint sold to coat the backs of hooked rugs. Theoretically, it prevents loops from pulling out and provides a nonskid backing. It is sticky and turns to cement with time, making future repairs impossible. Do not use this product.

Caring for Your Rug

Hooked rugs in low-traffic areas need little cleaning. A biweekly gentle vacuuming with a hand-held or canister vacuum cleaner (suction open) should be sufficient. Never use an upright vacuum cleaner or beater bars; the bristles will chew your rug to bits.

Vagrant threads should be clipped, not pulled. That thread is attached to a strip, which may pull out, leaving a bare patch in your rug. If you find cut ends peeking out on the underside of your rug, use a crochet hook or rug hook, to pull them back to the surface where they belong.

Dogs and cats seem to love to chew or claw hooked rugs. If this occurs, keep the pieces and repair the rug yourself, or send it to an expert (see Sources) if the job proves too onerous.

For serious soil, make a foam of a mild liquid detergent. Apply this foam with a cloth or sponge to clean the top surface of your rug. Do not soak the pile; it is important to keep the foundation from becoming saturated. Blot the foam to absorb the soil and moisture, and permit the rug to dry flat on an absorbent surface, such as a towel. Change the towel when it becomes damp to hasten drying. Do not hang the rug to dry as the weight of the damp fibers will weaken the foundation.

Hooked rugs can take a lot of wear, but be kind. They are rising in value every day, and the rug you wipe your feet on today may someday be a priceless antique.

Sources

Instructional video
Pat Hornafius
113 Meadowbrook Lane
Elizabethtown, PA 17022
(717) 367-7706
"How to Make a Traditional Hand Hooked Rug"
A complete description of rug making that includes planning the rug, hooking techniques, and hemming the finished rug. Equipment needed and sources are included.
60 minutes VHS
$30 U.S. plus $4.50 U.S. or $5 Canada (parcel post)

Patterns described in this book are available from

Harry M. Fraser Co.
R & R Machine Co., Inc.
433 Duggins Road
Stoneville, NC 27048
(910) 573-9830

Supplies

The sources listed here provide supplies for hooked rug making.

Most companies have catalogs, but please send along a self-addressed, stamped business-sized envelope for answers to inquiries from master dyers and wool suppliers.

Shirley Bloom

5486 S.R. 96 West
Shelby, OH 44875
(419) 347-5787
Master dyer, teacher, and supplier of wool swatches, spot dyed wool, and custom dyed wool.

Braid-Aid

466 Washington Street
Pembroke, MA 02359
(617) 826-2560
Complete hooking supplies.

Connie Charleson

9920 Weiskopf Drive
New Port Richey, FL 34655-2131
(813) 372-1010
Teacher and custom dyeing.

Cecilia Evans Clement

Fernwood Road Box 1978 Route 2
Cochranville, PA 19330
(610) 857-2628
Primitive hooked rug teacher and rug restoration.

DiFranza Designs

25 Bow Street
North Reading, MA 01864
(508) 664-2034
Red Dot Tracer (Red Dot Tracer is also available from fabric stores) and hooking supplies.

Dorr Mill Store
P.O. Box 88, Dept. RH
Guild, NH 03754-0088
(603) 863-1197 or (800) 846-3677
Complete rug hooking supplies and Dorr wools.

Dotti Ebi
501 Kingsburg
Dearborn, MI 48128
(313) 562-5156
Teacher, custom dyeing, spot dyeing, and wool supplier.

Forestheart Studio
200 South Main Street
Box 112
Woodsboro, MD 21798
(301) 845-4447
Linen rug backing and rug hooking supplies.

Harry M. Fraser Co.
R & R Machine Co., Inc.
433 Duggins Road
Stoneville, NC 27048
(910) 573-9830
Harry M. Fraser is the sole distributor of Pat Hornafius
rug patterns found in *Country Rugs, Victorian Cottage
Rugs,* and other publications. Bliss Strip Slitter and complete hooking suppies.

Fredericksburg Rugs
P.O. Box 649
Fredericksburg, TX 78624
(800) 331-5213
A complete line of rug hooking supplies and material.
Custom dyeing.

Ralph and Gloria Grey
4877 Ashworth Road
Mariposa, CA 95338
(209) 966-5888
Grey dye spoons, ranging from 1 teaspoon to $1/128$ teaspoon. These are essential for measuring PROChem dyes.

I. W. Designs
248 Outlook Drive
Pittsburgh, PA 15228
(412) 344-1257
The Pittsburgh Crafting Frame.

Maryanne Lincoln
139 Park Street
Wrentham, MA 02093
(508) 384-8188
Master dyer, teacher, and lecturer. Write to Maryanne Lincoln for hand-dyed wool for the patterns listed in *Victorian Cottage Rugs*.

Ramona Maddox
7108 Panavista Lane
Chattanooga, TN 37421
(615) 892-1858
Wetter than Water (Fuller product), available in 2-ounce and 8-ounce bottles.

Mandy's Wool Shed
Rt. 1, Box 2680
Litchfield, ME 04350
(207) 582-5059
Wool.

Mayflower Textiles
P.O. Box 329
Franklin, MA 02038
(508) 528-3300
Puritan rug frames.

Nancy Miller
2251 Ralston Road
Sacramento, CA 95821
(916) 925-8017
Miller Rug Hooking instruction and supplies.

Betty Morning
2419 Drexel Street
Vienna, VA 22180
(703) 560-2066
Teacher and custom dyeing.

Morton House Primitives
Kathy Morton
9860 Crestwood Terrace
Eden Prairie, MN 55347
(612) 934-0966
A full line of rug hooking supplies.

Joan Moshimer's Rug Hooker Studio
P.O. Box 351
21 North Street
Kennebunkport, ME 04046-0351
(800) 626-7847
Complete hooking supplies and Cushing dyes.

Jane Olson
P.O. Box 351
Hawthorne, CA 90250
(310) 643-5902
Master dyer and teacher. Rug supplies and swatches.
Write to Jane Olson for hand-dyed wool for the patterns
listed in *Victorian Cottage Rugs*.

J. D. Paulsen
P.O. Box 158
Bridgton, ME 14009
Rigby cutters.

Prisms or Prisms II
Claire de Roos and Nancy McClennan
302 Burbank Avenue
Johnson City, NY 13790
Master dyers and teachers. Dye formulas using PRO-Chem dyes. These pamphlets are available from Harry M. Fraser Co. and all rug suppliers.

PRO Chemical & Dye Inc.
Dept. RH, P.O. Box 14
Somerset, MA 02726
(508) 676-3838 or (800) 2-BUY-DYE (orders only)
PROChem WashFast Acid Dyes and Synthrapol wetting agent. Dye workshop, technical help, and free catalog.

Sweet Briar Studio
Janet Dobson
866 Main Street
Hope Valley, RI 02832
(401) 539-1009
Rug hooking instructions and supplies, rug restoration, custom dyeing. Janet Dobson can supply you with custom dyed wool used for patterns in *Victorian Cottage Rugs*.

Jessie Turbayne
P.O. Box 2540
Westwood, MA 02090
(617) 769-4798
Hooked rug restoration and cleaning.

Way Out West
P.O. Box 3094, Dept. RH
Carlsbad, CA 92009
(619) 929-0870 or (800) 326-8479
Rug Hugger. Send for a free brochure.

Index